FAITH

The Final Frontier

FAITH

The Final Frontier

By

David Alan Carmichael

A book from Majesty Publishing

Hampton, Virginia - 2004

FOREWORD

By Leslie Young Carmichael

As Mrs. David A. Carmichael, I would like to assure the reader that this journey chronicled here has been the most horrible, wonderful, terrifying and exciting time of my life. God has taken the two of us, and our four children, on the adventure of a lifetime. He took our anemic, atrophied faith and began to initiate us into the most rigorous training program imaginable.

God has asked us to do what we never wanted to do. He asked us to go where we never wanted to go. And eventually He asked us to, in effect, close our eyes, and jump off the cliff into his invisible hand.

Now you need to realize that my husband seems to relish this sort of adventure. Possibly, jumping off of cliffs is a rush for him. Not so for me. I like stability. I like continuity. I like predictability. Well, God had other plans for me. He decided to stretch, build and sharpen me. None of which are very pleasant for the one being stretched, built, and sharpened.

When I look at myself in the mirror each morning, there are certain reflections that I don't want to see. For instance, I don't want to see Jezebel, Martha, or Lot's wife looking back into my eyes. I like to think of myself more in terms of Esther, Ruth or Mary. In the past I would say my motto would have been "Be it unto me according to your word." But the testing of my faith in these past seven years has almost invariably evoked cries reminiscent of Job's wife. "What did you do to bring all this on us?" I would mutter to my husband through gritted teeth. Once, I am not proud to say, I even came close to quoting the embittered wife of Job when she said "Why don't you just curse God and die?"

The school of Faith is not an end in and of itself. It is training ground for the rest of life on Earth. I can say now in perfect honesty that "Once I heard of you, but now I have seen you with my own eyes." I believe God has brought the pot of my life to full boil because there were impurities that had to be removed. It is likely because of me and my resistance to change that He has had to keep the heat on. He has been faithful to bring reprieve periodically, but the heat remains high.

This narrative tells of some of the battles between flesh and spirit that we have wrestled with. It by no means tells them all. What I hope stands out to the reader is that God is trustworthy...all the time. He tests us, refines us and reshapes us in order to build Godly character in us, in order to use us.

I do not think God has ever doubted the Carmichael's desire to be used by Him for His purpose, but I think He realized He had a lot of work to do in us.

To simply obey has been the hardest task I have ever come up against. To submit without hearing from God personally, goes against my natural inclinations. I finally came to the conclusion that if God told David to do something that I thought was nutty, if I were to submit anyway, that I would score a 100 on my part of the test. Even if David was completely wrong and scored a zero, we would have a combined score of 50. Its not too great, but its better than a zero we would have received if he heard wrong and I rebelled too.

Every good story needs good characters, a conflict, climax and resolution. You've got to have a protagonist and an antagonist; a hero and a villain. Truly my husband has been the hero in faith and I the faithless villain. So if it seems like I appeared to be a naysayer, it is because in my history, it has been my knee-jerk reaction to tribulation.

I feel some remorse over this very human response. I take great hope, however, in the renewal of our minds that faith in God instills. I am not so quick to fear or doubt as I have in the past. The veil is being peeled back to reveal the unseen to my hungry eyes. I am learning to view the situations of my life with curious expectation rather than fearful dread.

It has been a privilege to feast on manna. Somehow what seems a simple fare is so sweet because of it's heavenly origin. Could I ever go back to the Egyptian banquet after living off of God's delicacy? I pray the Lord allow us to always have account to trust Him for something. Self-sufficiency is a plague that I want to forever avoid.

TABLE OF CONTENTS

Episode One

Introduction

A Still Small Voice

What would you do if, like some folks in the Bible, you heard God speak to you? Would you tell anyone?

Does God only speak to those who believe that He speaks? Moses did not know God. Yet, God revealed Himself and gave Moses a task that radically changed his vocation and lifestyle.

Consider that God most often spoke to people to tell them to do something that they were not naturally motivated to do.

Would you permit your life to be changed as a consequence of obedience?

One day, at the pinnacle of my career, I had to make that decision.

Episode One

In March 1997, I was a Surface Sonarman Chief Petty Officer in the United States Navy with nearly seventeen years of service. I had loved the path my career had taken and I had been able to accomplish things that very few of my peers had attained. With the proper amount of military discipline, I was motivated to give my best. I was promoted on the first round of consideration at each juncture from E-5 through E-6. At seven years, two months and five days of service, I put on the uniform of a Chief Petty Officer as an early candidate, four years before I would normally be eligible by time in service.

I was thrilled to put my training to good use. In fulfillment of all my hopes, I was eventually transferred to work on the staff of a Warfare Commander. My job was to plan anti-submarine training for the battlegroup that our unit was assigned to. Once we were at sea, my job evolved into planning the tactical use of various battlegroup units such as ships, aircraft, submarines and other assets. I had to plan communications; ship, submarine and aircraft search areas; submarine safety; unit formations; and I deciphered and disseminated meteorological and oceanographic information. Then, I would operate with the plan whenever it was my turn to stand the watch as the Undersea Warfare Commander Assistant Staff Watch Officer.

In the summer of 1996, I had the honor to stand the Tactical Watch Officer job for the Undersea Warfare Commander in the USS THEODORE ROOSEVELT Battlegroup during their final pre-deployment warfare exercises. My job was to make tactical decisions for things regarding "Anti-Submarine" warfare. This job was seldom given to an enlisted man when there are "qualified" officers available on the staff. The events themselves would make a good military adventure book. I performed well enough that a Navy Commendation Medal was being hurried through processing so that I could receive it before my quickly approaching transfer to my last shore duty before retirement. My prospects for promotion to E-8 looked very good. Then, God spoke, and everything changed.

One of the most difficult things to explain to anyone who has never had it happen to them, is how do you know God is speaking to you. Is it an audible voice you hear with your ears? Is it something you feel? Is it something that overwhelms your thoughts? If it is just an idea that comes to you, how do you know it is not just your own imagination?

I was once asked, "How do you know there is a God? Have you ever seen Him?" I could not let the opportunity get away to show that the Living God has a tangible presence and I have experienced it, though I had never seen Him with my eyes. My reply surprised him and turned his mocking into curious and awed wonder. I responded to his question, "...have you ever seen Him?" with a strong, though figurative, "Yes!"

You recognize voices of the people you know and especially those whom you love. The more time you spend with someone, the more easily you recognize their voice, even when there are many other noises and voices distracting your hearing. You learn to recognize voices by trial and error. When I first met Leslie Young, who is now my wife, I was just beginning to get used to her voice, with her southern Mississippi accent, when I met her sister Suzy. It was very difficult, at first, to recognize which 'Young' lady I had on the phone. I had to be very careful not to be too sweet to the person I was talking to until I was sure I knew I was speaking to Leslie.

During a youth camp where I was recently counseling, one of the campers asked their cabin leader, "How do you know there is a God?" She also asked, "How do you know when God is talking to you?" The leader brought Shellie to me thinking I might have some ideas. This teenager happened to have two identical twin brothers who, to everyone else, are very difficult to tell apart except for a few freckles. I asked Shellie, "When P.J. or Marcus walk up behind you and start speaking, can you tell which one it is without looking?" She replied with a definite "Yes!" I explained to her that she could recognize their voices only because she knew them extremely well.

God's voice is like that. I hear Him in my thoughts, I sense the prompting of the Spirit upon my heart and I recognize that the thought is not generated from my own personality. If the thought is from God, it is Biblically sound.

Sometimes God may speak to me to give me a task. A task that God gives, however, will not necessarily fit into someone else's Biblical formula. When God told Phillip to go travel the road that leads to Gaza from Jerusalem[1], He did not tell him why. There was not a clear Biblical context for him to measure the authenticity of the word. In fact, obeying the command would force him to shirk his Deacon responsibilities.[2] Had Phillip told someone, "I think God is calling me to travel the road to Gaza", they might have told Phillip that God would not tell him to do something that would cause him to

---

[1] *Acts 8:26-40*
[2] *Acts 6:1-7*

neglect his duties. Phillip must have been aware that on its face, God's command would seem to be contrary to the practice of a "mature" Christian. In hindsight, we know that Phillip <u>did</u> receive a word from the Lord. He was given an opportunity to share the gospel with an Ethiopian eunuch. Phillip's miraculous transport to a different place just after the eunuch's baptism authenticated the event as one that was ordained by God.

Look at a vision given to Peter while he was praying.[3] God showed Peter a bunch of animals that were unlawful for him to eat based upon the Biblical dietary code, and then told him, *"Rise, Peter; kill and eat."* Peter had no doubt that God spoke to him, yet he was confused because of his limited understanding. Peter refused, justifying his refusal on the basis of scripture. He said to the Lord in good faith, *"Not so, Lord! For I have never eaten anything common or unclean."* The Lord responded to Peter, *"What God has cleansed you must not call common."* Suddenly, and of course in a timely manner, he had an invitation to go take the gospel to a Gentile. The Holy Spirit then gave Peter understanding about the application of the vision and the word spoken by the Lord. As Peter

---

[3] *Acts 10*

obeyed, He saw God confirm His word through a miraculous work. The Gentiles were filled with the Holy Spirit. In my experience, when God speaks, He glorifies Himself and furthers His kingdom.

This book has true stories about times that I have received a word spoken directly by the Lord. In nearly each case, I struggled with the cost of obedience. In each case you will probably share my natural fears. Consider how you would react if the Lord gave you the same word. What would be at risk? What would you have to die to? What would your family say? What are the potential consequences of obedience? What are the physical and spiritual consequences of disobedience?

Most people will understand my wife's fears and knee-jerk reactions. Leslie, in most cases, did not get the benefit of sensing the power and presence of the Lord when she heard our new tasking. Yet, the potential negative consequences of my actions would have their greatest impact on Leslie and our children. Her faithfulness to yield to God's work, with the benefit of only hearsay evidence that it was God's will, may very well be why God has blessed us so much. Jesus said, "Blessed are those who have not seen, yet have believed."[4]

 I need to lay the groundwork for my readiness to hear from the Lord in the first part of this book. Like learning about the development of the faith and failings of the Apostle Peter, you will see how God mercifully allowed me to be used for His purposes in spite of my doubts. You will read about times when my thoughts, my words, and my actions were, inspired by the Holy Spirit. You will also see how I stumbled woefully. Yet, in each situation, God showed Himself strong as well as merciful. So, get ready for some demonstrations of God's obvious divine intervention. You will be encouraged by His miracles.

---

[4] *John 20:29*

Episode Two

Walking License Suspended

I experienced the tangible presence of God for the first time in August of 1975. I was a hoodlum in the making who had chocked-up a criminal record two years earlier at the age of eleven. At the age of thirteen, I was invited by a Christian youth group to attend summer camp at an American Baptist camp in Crestline, California. Their hope was to get me to this camp where I would hear about Jesus and possibly give my life to Him (get saved). I was excited about going to camp because of the prospect of having all kinds of girls I could meet who would not know my background. On Tuesday night of this camp, we went on an overnight hike. So far, my plan worked pretty well. I had made a hit with Miss (J.). Soon after the campsite was set up, my attention toward Miss (J.) was distracted as the group began to pray, sing, and worship, to the Lord Jesus Christ.

I began to sense the literal and tangible presence of the Holy Spirit. It was so obvious to me. I was awestruck and then stood in amazement that no one around me seemed to notice the incredibly forceful and powerful, yet gentle, Holy presence. The moment was surreal and is vividly etched in my memory now twenty-eight years later. My focus completely changed in response to God revealing Himself to me. The next morning, Miss (J.) found me to be completely disinterested in her. My attention was drawn to this presence of God I had experienced the night before.

I started really listening to the sermons during the camp chapel time. I realized that every word was important. I understood by the scriptures and the comfort given by the Holy Spirit that Jesus Christ is real. He came in the flesh, he died to suffer the consequences of my sin, He really did rise from the dead, and He is still living. Later that week I committed my life to Jesus Christ and invited Him to take over the lead of my life, to accept me and forgive my sin. All the youth group were astounded at the immediate and radical change that came over me. They all agreed that they had seen a miracle.

Prior to coming to know Jesus, I really had a limited concept of what was evil. I was certain that doing something to harm someone else was wrong. I knew that doing things reserved by law to adults, or against the law, were wrong; such as drinking alcohol, taking other drugs or viewing dirty magazines or movies. I knew that being disrespectful to any authority over me was also wrong. Beyond those things, I could do what I wanted as long as I got away with it. My language was vulgar and I was mean spirited. I had the audacity to publicly mock my teachers and fellow students in order to get laughs on shock value. I had a life-style of criminal behavior though I was caught and punished only once.

When I made Jesus Christ the ruler of my life, everything about my sinful character changed immediately. I became humble. My vulgar vocabulary vanished without any conscious effort. I actually forgot about vulgar things that I had ever said. My insatiable desire to do wrong things shifted to a desire to do what was right. However, like most new believers, I was left adrift. I had no idea what God expected of me except I knew that I was not supposed to sin. I understood right away, without having to be taught, that those things done contrary to God's will were sin. God had written His law in my heart.[5]

Not long afterward, I experience wrestling with temptation. I followed my flesh and took the path of least resistance. It happened when I was invited to an amusement park in the company of some adults. Two of them were U.S. Navy officers. The amusement park was also a brewery and adults could sample the brew. These two Navy men got beer samples and fed them to me. I knew it was breaking the rules. I rationalized that it was not inherently wrong to drink beer because it is legal. I was also tempted to not be a wimp in front of these fine American fighting men. I had not yet learned coping skills for such temptations. Even with my rationalizations, I knew it was wrong since I was under the legal age for alcohol consumption. I had enough to become drunk. The fine Navy officers had to keep close tabs on me to make sure they did not get into trouble.

The next day, I experienced some of the consequences of my sin when I had a pounding headache and nausea. I also reaped the consequences of guilt. I was ashamed of myself for doing what was wrong. I was grieved because God had forgiven me of my sin and my sinful life-style. Yet, I did what I knew was wrong, and I did it

---

[5] *Jeremiah 31:33-34; Hebrews 10:16*

publicly. How could I claim Christ as Lord to others and then disgrace Him openly through my actions. I <u>felt</u> that I disqualified myself from my newfound spiritual life. I <u>felt</u> stronger condemnation than I had when I had realized my sin prior to salvation. I lost that emphatic joy of a new believer.

Because of my internal shame, I drew away from Christ. I felt like Adam and Eve must have felt in the garden after they ate from the tree of the knowledge of good and evil. I drew away from those with whom I had just begun to establish fellowship at my Church. I began to hide from the things of God rather than seek them out.

Fortunately, I had already established a social activity regimen with my church. I was scheduled to go on a weekend retreat the week after Labor Day. I was somewhat subdued as I spent time with the people who I joined on the retreat. It was a weekend worship event where many dozens of youth groups got together for teaching, worship and fun. The Spirit of the Lord was there. My new nature that yearned for the things of God warred against my consciousness of the sin that I had committed. When I sensed the presence of the Lord during the worship services, I struggled internally with guilt. I had wavered in our intimate daily relationship. I grieved over not seeking

His company in the days leading up to the retreat. Yet, I <u>knew</u> that God loved me, and forgave me, and desired to have a close companionship with me. I sensed His love and forgiveness as well as His hope for my future.

During some of the sermons given that weekend, I heard the scripture 1 John 1:9. "If we confess our sin, God is faithful and just to forgive us our sins and to cleanse us from all unrighteousness." In my mind, it was hard for me to believe. But in my Spirit, I <u>knew</u> that it was true. I allowed the Lord to soften my heart and renew my spirit like the day of my salvation. However, I still hung on to guilt regarding what I considered as my betrayal of Christ.

Discipleship took a long time. Learning the wiles of Satan took time as well. During that time, Satan attacked with many weapons that I could not anticipate. I could not foresee the long-term consequences of letting down my guard or allowing myself to march alongside the enemy. The rate at which I succumbed to attack seemed to me much faster than my rate of spiritual development. Like many new believers, especially teenagers, it seemed to me that my spiritual high points were fleeting. The discouragement I felt over faltering hung on nearly perpetually.

Between 1975 and 1979, I repeated cycles of stumbling and then getting my act together. When I would come to my senses, repent of my most recent waywardness and spend time in prayer, I would get a renewed sense of forgiveness and hope. God's mercy is so great. When I was fervently walking faithfully, I found myself in a position of leadership where I had many opportunities to teach others and encourage them with the gospel and principles I had learned through some of my victories. The Lord's grace was sufficient to make others recognize His Spirit upon me. In the summer of 1979, I experienced the exhilaration and benefits of a right walk with the Lord Jesus. I had a lot of time to spend in prayer and Bible study. I made myself available to Him and He put me to good use. It was a summer of renewal for me. However, I was not wary of the cunning of our enemy Satan. I became prideful in my flesh regarding the "spiritual" things God had done through me. Like the week following my salvation in 1975, I again stumbled in sin shortly after my glorious mountaintop experience.

My first big calamity involved being led to a place of temptation by one my Christian peers. I was in a place where I could have either taken a stand for righteousness or at least fled for my spiritual life. I did neither. I allowed myself to be surrounded by the activities of a carnal crowd thinking I was immune from being poisoned by it. It is not necessary to detail the specific temptations or my sinful responses. It is critical though to point out their effects. Rightly so, I felt very guilty that I had not stood for Christ and urged my friends away from the assault on our innocence. Worse yet, we were no longer bound together by a fellowship in Christ but instead shared the knowledge that we had tainted ourselves with exposure to wickedness. I learned that it was not enough to refrain from the wicked activity. Letting my eyes fall on it was participation enough to desperately grieve the spirit and wound my soul. Rather than calling out to God for forgiveness, and then moving on from there with a sense of God's purpose in my life, I felt unholy and unworthy of the calling of Jesus Christ. I began a somewhat rapid spiritual downward spiral. I continued a downward trend until I got to a point in 1982 where I believed that I had gone too far to be redeemed. I felt spiritually dead.

Before the next chapter where I tell of the miraculous event that brought me around to getting on the right track, I want to explain what I learned about Satan's deception that was throwing me off course. I will use an analogy of a physically traumatic experience I had on

February 2, 2002.

I turned forty at the end of 2001. It is one of those milestones that are notorious for making us take a somber look at our mortality. As I approached my fortieth birthday, it was certainly obvious to me that I could not run as far, jump as high, lift as much or move as nimbly as I had been able to just a few years ago. Though I tried to outwardly play down my remorse as much as possible, I was dealing with a mild internal mid-life vitality crisis. To shake-off the nagging sense of decay, I took every little opportunity to do something vigorous (except of course anything truly considered deliberate exercise). On the fateful day of February 2, 2002, I accompanied my family to the YMCA to enjoy watching my youngest son Isaac (6½ years old) play a game of indoor soccer. The game had concluded and we were a bit rushed to make the next family activity, a Bible quiz for my oldest two children. I rushed my wife ahead of me so she could get the kids buckled into the car as fast as possible while I gathered our belongings. I stuffed my arms with jackets, spill-proof sports bottles and a nice, hot, tall cup of cocoa that I bought for my wife. I sort of power-walked to the front doors of the building. I could see through the glass doors that my wife was loading the kids into our mini-van that we had parked as close to the building exit as we could, knowing we needed to make a quick exit. There were several groups of people who had just exited the building a few yards ahead of me. I could see that the middle section of doors had not been used and I gloated that I would not have to break my hurried stride.

As I stepped through the door however, to my dismay, the groups of people on my left and right started drifting toward one-another and would converge just before I arrived if I kept the same pace. I would be trapped in a slower than casual pace for the remainder of my trip to the parking lot. It would make all my effort, to that point, a total waste. I had to act quickly if I wanted to preserve my investment. I leaped to a gallop at an oblique angle to my left through the tightening gap with just a slight brush upon one person and the swirl of my vortex on the other. Each of the eight or nine people walking in nearly a line with each other had to be quite startled as I suddenly burst out in front of them. In my thoughts that were contemplated at the speed of light, I knew that I ought to be humiliated for my action. I considered slowing abruptly to resume my prior pace. It occurred to me that my obnoxious burst through the crowd could not be justified, unless the cause of my hurry demanded a continuing rush to meet my unpublished emergency. So, I had to keep up my pace to keep up the façade. The next split second brought the realization that I ought to be thoroughly humiliated. After all, I am forty, dressed fairly nicely, balding, graying, with arms full of stuff, and I had no emergency that could justify my impetuous behavior. My counter thought was, "Who cares?" "There is a cloudless and blue sky. The sun is bright. The air is brisk. I am forty, but I feel good!" Upon concluding my split-second contemplation, I accelerated.

Because I was moving at such a high velocity, I had to turn my head to the right to see if there were any cars coming way before I was anywhere near the parking lot. I had just reached the apex of my speed and suddenly I was transported into a much less exhilarating experience. A sharp and strong burst of pain shot from my left toe and was felt throughout my entire being. My arms were suddenly empty and my head, face, arms and chest were baptized in warm cocoa. My speed did not change, only my trajectory. As my body was being whipped toward the ground as if my feet were a hinge, my split second sequential thoughts were: "What was that? Ooooh, I hit something that I didn't see. Man! This is going to be embarrassing. I wish I had not already drawn everyone's attention. Ooooh, Man!

Episode Two

This is going to hurt bad!!!"

Sure enough! I have never experienced such physical trauma in my entire life, and I may never experience such again. Some silly person had put a huge steel bike-rack in the pathway and I had not noticed it in my nearsighted awareness of the human blockade, and in my far-sighted glances into the parking lot. My left foot made the initial impact and my right foot hooked itself under the slightly upturned bike-rack frame. My knees, arms, thighs, elbows, left shoulder and head hit with such rapidity that it probably looked simultaneous. I drew blood at each point of impact. I felt an excruciating rush of pain, head to toe and front to back. Even my organs hurt. I was severely winded and extremely slow to recover the ability to draw a breath. I was faintly aware of the horrific gasp that escaped each of the on-lookers. I was readily aware that they hurriedly surrounded me in their desire to rescue me from my calamity.

Though I was traumatized beyond the ability to function, I had many natural reactions that would motivate me to make things appear as if there was nothing wrong.

Firstly, I felt bad for those around me who no doubt expected better of me than my throwing my body into a mass of steel. I am sure they could not have any idea what would motivate me to do something that was so self-destructive.

Secondly, I was humiliated beyond imagination and wanted desperately to be able to put on a show of normalcy in the hopes that my witnesses could speedily lose the mental picture of my downfall.

As I lay there, entangled in steel bars, I desperately wished I could get up, brush myself off, and prove to myself and my observers that I was able to move on and walk normally. But I couldn't. I had to admit it. I could not even move. All I could do was lay there. I did not know if my dysfunction was temporary or if I would have to be carried away. But for the sake of my survival, humiliation was the least of my worries. I was subject to the consequences of my false step. Whatever had to be done to raise me up, was just par for the course. I would have to accept any disability that resulted from my error.

Most important in this incident of physical stumbling is what I did **not** do. Imagine the absurdity of my lying there and making the following contemplation:

'Man! I blew it. I was doing what I felt like doing, all the while knowing it was stupid. Worse yet, I did it right in front of everybody.

I got what I deserve.' (So far, not so bad)

'Don't even think about getting up David. Don't even think about trying to act like you can walk. Who do you think you are going to fool? Everyone saw you fall. Everyone will know that you are a faker. Everyone will know you are a stumbler. Everyone will know you can't walk. If you even try to walk, they're just going to think that you are putting on another show. You will just be a hypocrite.' (More than a hint of absurdity)

'In fact, since everyone knows you can't walk, any attempt you make to act like you can walk will just cause you to get in the way of those who really do know how to walk. It will be better for your sake, and theirs, if you just stay down and roll out of the way so you do not impede anyone else with your stumbling.'(Just downright ridiculous)

It would be pretty unreasonable to have that line of thinking in the instance of a physical accident. It would be permanently debilitating beyond the actual damage caused by the catastrophe. It is easy to see on a physical plane that it is a thought process that is unreasonable.

In the physical realm, it is more reasonable to rest as long as is needed to recover from the damage of the injury; to get whatever therapy is necessary to walk functionally again; and to avoid situations in the future that would risk such a fall. You may even tell others what happened to you so they can learn from your mistake instead of having to experience injury themselves. I certainly experienced enough pain to make me fear ever trying to jog again. Appropriately, my rational mind did it's job and forced me to recuperate and resume running (only whenever and where ever appropriate though).

In my spiritual life, I stumbled and fell through sin. When I fell, I was shocked. I had not expected it. I expected myself to be perfect. Since I had stumbled in front of others, I told myself that I should not even try to walk in Christ because then I would just be a faker. I made myself believe that because I had stumbled, it proved I was not really able to walk in Christ. Since others had seen me stumble, they would consider me a hypocrite if I attempted to walk in Christ. I felt like I should not get up once I stumbled. I considered that my trying to act like I could walk in Christ would just cause interference in the lives of those who were really able to do it. I would just end up causing them to stumble over me. I gave in to the accusations of Satan and I began to give up.

Episode Two

I never actually lost my true identity as one who belongs to Christ. When I came to the Lord, He changed me. I did nothing to change myself. He gave me a new nature that was trapped inside my old body. I had truly been born anew by the Spirit of the Living God.

It is very easy for an unbeliever to understand that we are not qualified to "walk in Christ." When I came to Christ, I understood fully that there was nothing in me that could classify me as being worthy of His love. I came to Him completely disqualified. There was nothing I could do to make the situation any better and there was nothing else I could do to make it any worse. The only thing that was required of me was to acknowledge my unworthiness, to recognize His Holiness, and to receive Him for my forgiveness. The word of God says, "He came to His own and His own did not receive Him. But as many as received Him, to them He gave the right to become children of God, even to those who believe in His name."[6] Even though I was completely disqualified, I had the power to become a child of God on the basis of my "receiving Christ", because of Christ's sacrifice and love for me. After receiving Him and becoming a child of God, my duty then is to "walk in Him." "Therefore, as you have

---

[6] *John 1:11-12*

received Christ Jesus the Lord, so walk in Him."[7]

I did not understand as a new believer that it is not the balance of my sin versus my abstinence of it that qualifies me. It is only on the basis of the relationship that He established with me. Let's admit it, "If we say that we have no sin, we deceive ourselves and the truth is not in us."[8]   But, "If we confess our sins, He is faithful and just to forgive us our sin, and to cleanse us from all unrighteousness."[9]

Sin does not suspend our license to walk with Christ: It certainly brings injury when we stumble; it embarrasses those around us who see our stumbling; we have pain and grief until we recover from the injury of our error; somebody who watches us fall may be rightfully hesitant to pass us the baton to join them in the race they are running; but we do not lose our status. What is critical for us to do, is to readily admit our sin, confess it and allow God to cleanse us from it. Then, just as we received Him, walk in Him. Our God wants us to be over-comers. He wants to show His glory through us, His apparently imperfect but favored children.

---

[7]   *Colossians 2:6*
[8]   *1 John 1:8*
[9]   *John 1:9*

Episode Three

A Nice Trip

After, I made myself available to the Lord in the summer of 1979, my soul was soothed by the sense of identity in Jesus Christ and of His presence with me. I experienced the fulfillment of His promise, "Come to me, all you who are weary and burdened, and I will give you rest."[10] Christ was faithful to restore our relationship after my young teenager stumbling. He put me to good use in His kingdom. However, I reaped the fruit of the seeds I sowed of irresponsibility and of wasting time. I had not earnestly pursued a discipleship regimen in my relationship with the Lord Jesus Christ. My relationship style was one of a cycle of error and apology. In any human

---

[10] *Matthew 11:28 (HCSB)*

relationship, like in business and agriculture, investment of resources is an absolute necessity for a healthy and vital outgrowth. Likewise, a healthy relationship with Christ is one that grows as a result of deliberate nurturing. Like in a marriage, communication is the means and intimacy is the end.

Because of my neglecting to behave wisely as a disciple of Christ, I had not learned to avoid pitfalls that are built into life's path. I was not keenly aware of the battle that is being waged for my soul in the heavens. I was not aware of how powerfully we can be distracted and deceived by subtle natural yearnings. Wanting in my person to do good, and seeing how the Lord had used me, I made myself vulnerable. I found myself becoming influenced by others rather than me influencing them for Christ. Then, the old cycle of stumbling returned, but this time it was more grave. I developed a pattern of wrong behavior that seemed to be innocent at first. I could not see that Satan was luring me into a web. When I realized I had let myself become prey, I gave in and I gave up. I, like never before, had temptation to abandon morality. Why not? I believed I had disqualified myself from my inheritance as a child of God. To what extent I had participated in the revelry of the common man is not important. I had acted worse than some and not as bad as others. My acts were predicated on my belief that all was lost. Why do good (denying my flesh) unless doing good had a tangible benefit? Certainly any hope for eternal benefit was lost. I began to live a life typical of those who have no life in Christ.

Fortunately, I was deeply grieved by every wrong thing that I did. Innately, I knew who I was (a child of God). I knew where I should be (walking alongside Christ). But I could not conceive how to escape my bondage. Jesus said, "I assure you, everyone who commits sin is a slave of sin…"[11]

In the summer of 1982, I was transferred to a Navy school in San Diego for a little over a year. It was a chance for me to exercise a little freedom rather than what seemed like captivity living on a ship. I responded to some ads in the paper where people were renting out spare rooms in their homes. Sailors seem to be the lowest caste in San Diego. I was shunned everywhere I applied. So, I started driving around the Ocean Beach community looking for an apartment to rent. I wanted to acquire a two-bedroom apartment and then put an ad in the newspaper for somebody else to share the rent.

---

[11] *John 8:34 (HCSB)*

I drove by an apartment building that my brother used to live in and saw a sign advertising one of the apartments for rent. I called the landlady and she met me there right away. When we talked together, it seemed that I was being shunned again. I had no renter history and no credit. She started to put me off. Then she asked if I was related to Richard Carmichael. When I told her that he was my brother, you would have thought I wasn't a sailor. She suddenly treated me like she and I were family. Richard was the best renter she ever had. I was a shoe-in.

I placed an ad in the paper and the first guy that showed up to answer the ad seemed to be okay. Rod was a student finishing his teaching degree and had a steady job, steady income from a trust, and a good attitude. We got to be friends very quickly. Rod on the surface seemed that shallow party-hardy stereotypical Southern California beach culture type. He used the façade, like most people do, to bury the real man God intended him to be. Rod, had at one time experienced the presence of the Holy Spirit, he understood his sinful state and was being called to submit to Jesus Christ. He counted the cost and had very consciously rejected Christ's offer of salvation and eternal life. Rod knew his state and was satisfied with it.

He lived a life of wanton immorality, pursuing wine and women. He pragmatically contented himself with the short-lived thrills of sin and he tolerated their, admittedly negative, long-term consequences.

Rod was also very astute. He perceived, right away, the internal struggle I was having. He could see my underlying character and knew that God must have once done a real work in my life. He could see through my vain attempts to put on a worldly front. My misery was obvious to him. One day, Rod confronted me with a sharp reproof. He said, "David! You have a real problem. You keep trying to be a bad guy but you can't do it. Deep down, you are really a good guy but you can't bring yourself to live that way. You have a real problem. You better figure out what you are going to do. You need to come to a decision. What are you going to be,… good,… or bad?"

His question hit me right between the eyes. I was found out. When I considered the thought of what it would take to really become innately bad, I realized that it was a place that was just too far for me to go. I knew that the only real hope for my being able to experience happiness was to become "good" again. But how could that be? I had come to the place where I understood that I did not have the power within myself to be "good." Yet, I knew, "good" is what God wanted me to be. Little did I understand that God had just brought the prodigal[12] to his senses.

In July, 1983, I was coming to the conclusion of my year of Advanced Electronics Field training. I was living my daily routine of getting up around 10:00 a.m., going to Fleet Anti-Submarine Warfare Training Center to play volleyball with the lunch-time aficionados, and then buying a delicious submarine sandwich at Regatta's on Rosecrans Boulevard. I spent the remaining afternoon bodysurfing at Ocean Beach before going to my classes on base at night. Talk about having your cake and eating it too!

One day, I stayed a bit longer than I thought I should at the beach. When I thought that I would be hard-pressed to make muster on time, I hurriedly gathered my towel and cooler, and I headed for my apartment about 250 yards away. I assumed my fastest pace with my longest strides. Suddenly, a thought came to my mind to turn forty-five degrees to my right. It seemed so urgent that it overrode my concern of being tardy. As soon as I turned though, I completely

---

[12] *From Jesus's parable about a wayward son returning to his father. Luke 15*

forgot what motivated my urgent course change to starboard. I looked at the storefronts in the new direction I was headed, hoping it would remind me of why I was headed there. It was like times when we find ourselves entering a room of our house without knowing what drew us there. If we pause long enough to think about it, we usually figure it out. In this case, nothing in my mind or in my view gave me a clue about the purpose of my trek. I considered abandoning the project, but I fought the urge since it seemed so important for me to turn from my path in the first place. I decided that I had just better continue my path (as fast as possible) presuming that my mission would dawn upon me the closer I got to my objective.

I was cruising along as close to a jog as possible, while still having two feet on the ground. Suddenly, I tripped on what I could tell was someone's foot. I fell headlong and had to let go of my belongings so that my hands would be free to catch myself when I hit the ground. On my way down, I could see the body of the person who's left foot I had just tripped over. I caught myself at the lower end of a push-up position. My face was so close to the ground that the sand was dusted into my face from the swirl of air pressure made by my head's approach. As I was reeling from the onslaught of sand in my face, I heard the sound of sand falling in large quantities all over the person next to me. My sense of humiliation is indescribable. I could not imagine the pain they might be feeling because of my kick. I could easily imagine their discomfort of having a deluge of sand ruin their blissful respite in the late afternoon sun. Before I turned to address them, I tried to think of something to do or say that might lessen the offense of my battery. I concluded quickly that there was no hope of salvaging their comfort with humor or any other thing. A hearty and effusive apology was the only thing to give, knowing that anything else might incite blows.

With a look of heartfelt regret, I turned to my victim to beg forgiveness. To my astonishment, I knew the man. After we stared a moment at each other, I said, "Fred! What are you doing here?" With a questioning look on his face, Fred told me, "I don't know. What are you doing here?" Of course I replied, "I live here." Then Fred startled me when he said, "I live here too." I told Fred that I wished I could stop and talk with him but I was going to be late for muster and I had to hurry and walk up the street to my apartment to get ready. He said he lived a couple of blocks away and that he would walk with me to my house so we could visit on the way. I was thrilled at the opportunity. Fred Snider was somebody who I admired greatly. He was my camp counselor in 1975 and Fred was the primary person whom God used to bring me to Christ. I was very curious to know why I had not seen Fred at the beach before that moment. He told me he had moved into his apartment that day and that it was the same distance from the beach as my apartment. Fred interviewed me about my life since we last saw each other several years earlier. I was rather candid with him about my spiritual state. I asked him to come in to see my apartment and continue visiting with me while I got ready for work. When we got to my apartment, the clock showed that I was not late. I actually had some time to visit.

I escorted Fred in and gave him a seat in the kitchen where I offered him something to drink. Immediately, my roommate Rod came in from his day at work. I introduced Fred to Rod and explained how Fred was instrumental to my coming to know Christ years before and how I had tripped over him at the beach. Rod's facial expression changed to a bit of wonder and investigative curiosity. Rod perceived that my literally running into Fred was no coincidence. Rod, who usually evaded sticking around in the company of my friends, could not help himself but join me in hosting

Fred. After the introductions, I went about my task of obtaining Fred's refreshment while Rod interviewed him about our acquaintance. When I looked into the refreshment options, I found that it was a choice between, orange juice, tea, water and Coors beer. I reasoned that the later was probably not something Fred would consider but I offered it to him anyway. He accepted one of the other options. Trying to see if it was taboo for him, I mentioned that he probably did not even consider the beer. He stayed neutral on the subject but told me that he abstained from alcohol on the principle that it may be a stumbling block for other people who observe him.

I went over the tripping incident for Rod in detail for its entertainment value. When I got to the part where Fred responded to my question of what he was doing there, I asked him what he meant when he said he did not know. Fred told us a story that has had a huge impact on my desire to really live by faith. Fred said that he had a good job and a vibrant ministry. One day, God told him to go to San Diego. He questioned the Lord as to what he was supposed to do in San Diego but God did not tell him. As he continued to pray, he understood that God wanted him to quit his job, resign from his ministry, and move to San Diego. So, he told his wife, quit his job, resigned from his ministry, and they moved to San Diego. So there he was in San Diego, not knowing why. Rod's jaw dropped, he shook is head and left the room as if he had something he needed to do. I did not wonder too much at what Fred said. I knew him and had heard a few of his stories of God speaking to him. It just seemed to fit right in with the character I knew.

Fred had to get home and I had to get to school. Before he left, Fred invited Rod and me to come to dinner on another night. I called Rod out of his room to hear the invitation. He declined saying that it was best that Fred and I have a chance to renew our acquaintance without his distraction. After Fred left the apartment, Rod came alive with exultant admonishment. With "Aha!" in his expression, he waved his finger at me and said, "You better watch it! God is after you buddy. He's got your number. You can't tell me this is just a coincidence. I'm glad for you. You go and have a good time." As I said, Rod was astute.

I walked to Fred's apartment on the appointed evening. It was great to see his wife Dawn again. She is a beautiful lady with a vibrant zeal for the Lord. Fred was kind of rascally looking with crazy curly red hair and wild eyes. Dawn was pretty and poised, with a calm and soothing countenance. They are a pair that you would not naturally put together looking at the exterior, but you would not expect otherwise knowing their character. We had spaghetti, salad, and garlic bread. I ate abundantly, but not ferociously, while I interviewed the two of them about their lives since we had last seen each other. When I had about cleaned my plate, Fred said to me, "David. What happened to you eight years ago? Was it real? Did you really get saved? After the things you've told me, I wonder if you ever really had a relationship with Christ." His sudden conversation shift was rather startling but it was completely appropriate and timely.

I think Fred's question was the only question that I needed to consider regarding my spiritual state. I had let myself be discouraged thinking about each moment that I had failed the Lord. I kept thinking of my qualifications in Christ depending on the daily state of my heart. When I failed, I felt far from the Lord. However, Fred was not asking me how I felt about my spiritual state on that very day, as if it had anything to do with whether or not I was a child of God. He asked the most pertinent question. Did God really do a work in my life in August of 1975?

I paused, for not a very long while, to consider Fred's question.

It was very easy for me to come up with the truthful answer. The answer was, "Yes!"

I then began to tell Fred and Dawn about the state of my soul prior to going to camp that year. I told him about the incident where I sensed the presence of the Holy Spirit on the overnight hike. I explained to him how the word of God began to sink deep into my heart and mind from that point forward. I told him how I had come to the place on August 25, 1975 where I knew I had to make a choice between submitting to Christ as my Lord or rejecting Him. I had not ever before really been put in a situation where I had to explain the depth of my salvation experience. As I recalled the details, I began to sense the presence of the Lord again like I had on that day of my salvation. I began to recall not only in my mind, but in my spirit as well, the life changing work that God was doing during those moments I was counting the cost of yielding to the Lordship of Christ. Then I began to recall an interesting phenomenon I experienced as I sat in the pew pondering that I needed to get up and go forward during the invitation back in 1975.

I was in a state of prayer with my head bowed and my eyes closed. Amazing Grace was being sung as the invitation anthem. I had already come to the place where I knew that choosing Christ was my only realistically sound option. But I was not inclined to get up and walk forward into a group of strangers. I understood it was something I ought to do, but I was rationalizing in my mind whether it was really necessary. While I was praying and struggling over whether I would get up or stay put, I felt the sensation of two large warm hands on my back as if I was being coaxed to get up and go forward to the altar. I was immediately perturbed and turned around to send the person behind me a look that showed that they better keep their hands off of me. Surprisingly, all I saw was two younger girls sheepishly waiting for the conclusion of the service. I was startled to see them sitting there so meekly. They obviously could not support the large hands I had felt and they no doubt had not been touching me.

Contemplating the incident distracted me from my prayers because of its strangeness. I shuddered a bit and quickly turned back to my prayer position. I deliberated the need to actually move out of my seat to inaugurate my salvation. I came to the conclusion that it was necessary for me to walk forward if I was really serious about receiving Christ as Lord. The music was soon coming to a close and I knew it was then or never, but I still had a sense of humiliation that was tempting me to stay in my seat. Even with that temptation to stay, I had an understanding that I would forever regret a decision to not go forward. Then I felt the hands again. I knew rationally that there were no actual hands on my back. I knew that the hands were big and that the two timid young ladies behind me did not have the audacity for such an act. But I had to admit it. I felt hands on my back that gave me a sense of peace, yet seemed to be urging me out of my seat. It occurred to me that the hands belonged to Fred Snider. I looked up and saw Fred sitting on a bench in front of the pews to my right. He was just sitting there, facing the center of the altar area, with a kind of contemplative look on his face. You could tell he was kind of drifting in and out of prayer.

The hands were not physically Fred's, and I did not think there were really any hands on me. I did realize though that God wanted me to get up. I had internally given in, and I was going to get up, but I had to give one last look behind me to verify someone was not touching me. I turned around and found the two young ladies in prayer. My thought was, "Well! That does it!" I got up, went forward to the foot of the stage, and hung around the folks responding to the invitation.

At first I just kind of looked around waiting to be given instructions on what to do next. Then very suddenly, I felt a complete release of all my sin. I felt as if a huge weight had literally been lifted from my shoulders. I felt clean inside. I felt the love of God tangibly. I felt what I now know as joy. I knew instantly that I belonged to God. I experienced eternal liberty.

When I concluded recalling the story to Fred and Dawn, Fred continued to look at me rather stoically but Dawn had her mouth agape and said, "Wow! That's really neat!" She was very excited. She went on to explain that it seemed God really had done something special for me. She told me that Fred often prays for people and their salvation. When he does, he puts his hands out in front of him as if he were laying his hands on the person he is praying for. Her declaration made me kind of wince. It struck me how important I must be to God that He would use such an extraordinary supernatural work to prod me into the right behavior.

Fred then asked me what happened that had sent me into a wayward path. I told him about my stumbling in sin and the discouragement that it brought to me. I also told him about the times that God worked powerfully through me despite my cycle of stumbling. As I recalled the things that sent me off track and the mercies of the Lord setting me aright, I began to understand that I really was a child of the living God. Yet, I had allowed Satan to deceive me in his attempts to destroy me. With this realization, I openly confessed my sin to God before Fred and Dawn. With the confession came the realization of God's forgiveness. I experienced again a heavy burden being released from my soul. I felt liberated. As Jesus said, "Most assuredly, I say to you, whoever commits sin is a slave of sin. And a slave does not abide in the house forever, but a son abides forever. Therefore if the Son makes you free, you shall be free indeed."[13]

During my encounter with Fred and Dawn Snider, the Prodigal returned home. I encountered my Father's endless mercy and love. I was restored with full honors. I understood that I have the right to be called a child of the Living God. I knew that nothing could separate me from my Father's love.

In only a few weeks, upon the completion of my training, I was transferred out of San Diego to the East Coast. I looked forward to it being a time where I could start over with a new life, not haunted or

---

[13] *John 8:34-36*

daunted by those things that caused me sin and grief. Interestingly, I heard through the grapevine that Fred and Dawn moved away from San Diego in only a couple of months. It seems that God told Fred to quit everything and move to San Diego only to find there was not anything there for him. Is it possible that God told Fred and Dawn to move to San Diego so that Fred could begin accomplishing his mission on the first day of his arrival?

Mission accomplished!

Episode Four

Disciples Indeed

Upon regaining my hope in the summer of 1983, I earnestly desired a right walk in Christ. I was determined to shed those things that led to destruction, and embrace those things that led to life. I committed myself to regular church attendance and spiritually healthy relationships. My move to the East Coast was very instrumental to helping me stay on track with that pursuit. Whereas on the West Coast, I found myself surrounded by stumbling blocks and discouraging reminders of past falls.

Hampton Roads, Virginia, held a breath of fresh (though somewhat humid) air. I had been given a point of contact at a church in Hampton. I contacted Brother Donald Boone, who told me where to meet him for evening services at Phoebus Baptist Church. When I entered the building that night, I discovered a place full of the life of Christ. The people had the joy of the Lord and they loved me as Christ calls us to love one another. The Pastor, Leonard D. Riley, preached the word of God with power and without compromise. I found a congregation that was pursuing the things of God.

I quickly tried to place myself in fellowship with other believers who had a hunger for the Lord. I was there only a few weeks before I had to leave. My ship was transferred from the port of Norfolk, Virginia to a shipyard in Pascagoula, Mississippi. While in Mississippi, God led me to my perfect complement. Leslie and I were drawn together by our mutual desire to grow in Christ. We were married on December 29, 1984.

The day of our wedding, we began driving to our first home, in Norfolk, Virginia where my ship had returned after its overhaul in Pascagoula. While in Virginia, we received superb teaching from the staff at Restoration Church (Phoebus Baptist). In 1986, we had the opportunity to attend a seminar that is now called Institute in Basic Life Principles. The presentation was not necessarily captivating, but the message went to the bone. With nearly every teaching point presented in the seminar, Leslie and I learned how far we were from where we wanted to be spiritually. We desperately wanted to apply God's word in every aspect of our lives. The first day of the seminar was the first day of a rapid growth spurt in our faith. There were many things we changed in our habits. We began to tithe faithfully. I assumed the responsibility for our financial management. We spent more time in prayer together. We took each situation that came up and found the Biblical solution that applied. If there was a choice between our rational reasoning as a solution to a problem, and a principle of God's word that conflicted with our reasoning, we deliberately chose the Biblical solution, even to our hurt (seemingly). We experienced life more abundantly. We became excited about each opportunity to apply God's word. In my daily life, my witness for Christ became much stronger.

When we started to put God's word into daily practice, we discovered what Jesus meant by taking up your cross daily and following Him. Our innate desires are contrary to the methods of God. When we became aware of the word of God, we became hyper-aware of the temptations to go against it. When we actually put the principles of God's word into practice, we stuck out like sore thumbs. God's principles worked in many ways to bring peace in otherwise hostile environments. We also became stumbling blocks to those who did not know Jesus.

In the United States Navy, I had many challenges to my walk in Christ every day. I was bombarded with profanity. Others were deliberately offending me as part of the Navy societal norm. Because of my commitment to apply the word of God in every situation, I had the challenge of having to stand on God's word even to the point of being an offense while trying not to be an offender. Leslie and I prayed on the morning of my first day at a new duty station, Fleet Anti-Submarine Warfare Training Center, Atlantic, where I was to be an instructor. We prayed that I would have an opportunity to start my day off right, to establish myself as a man of Christ, and be well received at the same time.

I went to my new office where there were dozens of men ranking from E-5 to E-8. They were of the standard surly bunch that you would expect from a group of career sailors. I was greeted warmly and felt readily accepted. I went in applying the principle, "Even a fool is counted wise when he holds his peace."[14] Within a few dozen minutes of being in the office, one of the men, in a gesture of friendship

---

[14] *Proverbs 17:28*

and inclusion, attempted to initiate me into the resident fellowship by telling me a "Why did the…?" Joke. I predicted that the answer was probably going to be vulgar and so I, being on my guard, in a state of prayer, sought some sort of wisdom from the Lord on what to do. Staying silent would not be the thing to do. Stalling for time and maintaining a friendly air, I went along saying, "I don't know! "Why did the (subject) do (verb)?" Beyond my prediction, (D.)'s response was horrendously gross. My countenance dropped as a reflex. Laughing was not even something I was capable of doing because of the contrary effect his comment had on my soul. He, however, gave a big grin and looked forward to my taking pleasure in his jest. His countenance fell when he saw my reaction. A bit downtrodden, he asked me, "What's the matter? Didn't you like the joke?" Internally, I struggled with, "How do I not make him take it as a personal attack that I can't enjoy the vulgarity?"

The straightforward approach was the best route to take. I said with my most earnest and apologetic expression, "Please take no offense personally, but I am one of those radical Christians and I can't bring myself to take pleasure in those kind of jokes." His eyebrows and eyelids jumped up in a look of wonder. Then he just shrugged his shoulders and said, "Oh! Okay!" His natural happy countenance returned to him and he went on about his business. You must know also, as I did, that every ear in the room was tuned-in to the encounter.

It was a step of faith. I needed to align myself with Christ publicly from the outset. From that point onward, everyone would have certain expectations for my behavior. I also had subliminally given an invitation for others to open a dialog with me about Christ. My statement made some in the room wary of me. It put me at a disadvantage with my new leadership who, for the most part, were distrustful of someone who would take such a bold stand. They knew that my loyalty was to something higher than the Navy. Yet, they did not understand that my allegiance to God motivated me to faithfulness to the Navy and respect for its leaders.

At the same time, there was a man in our division, (E.), who was well known for being outspoken for Christ. However, his approach was to blast the staff with sermonettes about their wicked hearts. He portrayed himself as being righteous before God in contrast to his hell bound co-workers. He gave everybody a sense of the sermons he was hearing on Sunday morning but not necessarily a sense of the character of God. Rather than communicating the word and love of God, (E.) ostracized himself and just chalked it up as persecution.

I took a different approach to communicating my faith that showed itself to be very effective. Instead of pointing out everybody else's failure to meet God's standards, I concentrated on making sure that my words and deeds conformed to them. When I was challenged with some controversy I tried to answer my antagonist with the word of God, and it's requirements of <u>me</u>, rather than accuse them. In doing so, I found out that it worked as if 'I was rubber and they were glue. Whatever I said bounced off of me and stuck on (them).'

In one incident, one of the two primary office hecklers was complaining about a particular female Lieutenant who was in charge of him on a particular day of duty. He was assaulting her character and then caught himself realizing that public slander of a superior officer is obviously totally contrary to military protocol. Petty Officer (D.) feebly camouflaged his insubordination by making an appeal that he was only expressing an opinion of her personality and not of her rank or office. He began to solicit others to join him in his 'opine-fest'. Carefully avoiding the glances of the Senior Chief Petty Officers docked on the far isle of the room, he called out to others in the office, of his rank or below, whom he believed would candidly berate the absent officer. Sure enough, each one guardedly insulted the officer keeping within the fictitious boundaries of their little game. This same heckler often came to me with all sorts of strange controversies and then harassed me with frivolous questions. He would do it to set me up for a verbal sin or to mock my viewpoint if I gave a Biblical answer. It was obvious that he would eventually ask me for my opinion of LT (M.).

Sure enough, Petty Officer (D.) made a huge deal of coming to me for the final judgment. "DAAAAVVVEE! What's your opinion of Lieutenant (M.)?" I knew that giving any negative insight was certainly not to be considered. I also knew that making a compliment to counterbalance his onslaught would not be effective. It would raise hearty ridicule that would distract from any redeeming value. I called out to God for wisdom. The wisdom from God had already been supplied through scripture. Claiming the scripture for myself I said, "In a multitude of words sin is not lacking, but he who restrains his lips is wise!"[15] To my horror, Petty Officer (D.) almost doubled over as if he had been hit in the diaphragm. He understood perfectly that the

---

[15] *Proverbs 10:19*

51

opposite of a wise man, is a fool. His predominant personality characteristic, a man of many words, bared his plight.

I poured out apologies in futility. There was no hope for my recovery. He maintained his dazed look of suffocation. He waved off my pleadings for tolerance and my assurance that I meant no insult to him. There was nothing I could do. "For the word of God is living and effective and sharper than any two-edged sword, penetrating as far as to divide soul, spirit, joints, and marrow; it is a judge of the ideas and thoughts of the heart. No creature is hidden from Him, but all things are naked and exposed to the eyes of Him to whom we must give an account.[16]"

After being at my instructor job for about a year-and-a-half, I came upon the date that I received my annual performance evaluation. I had worked very hard and felt like I had earned a strong evaluation, though I did expect an evaluation that was weaker than my performance. My supervisors did not treat me as warmly as they treated my peers. I got along well with my seniors and my peers, and I had earned their respect. However, I had occasions when I really irritated my superiors by not doing unethical (and sometimes illegal)

---

[16] *Hebrews 4:12-13 (HCSB)*

things that they asked of me. I had a collateral duty to collect donations for the Combined Federal Campaign. One of the rules of the CFC is that no one will be harassed if they do or do not give. There was a rule that I was not allowed to give a list of names of contributors to anyone but the campaign coordinator. One day, our Senior Chief of the Division asked me to give him a list of the people who did, and did not, give. He wanted to pressure the non-givers to change their way so the division could show one hundred percent participation. Such a tactic is the norm. I respectfully refused on the basis of the orders I had from higher authority. The Senior Chief was very perturbed. Another time, I was ordered to change the travel claim I had submitted. They wanted me to lie about my expenses so that the rest of the group that went on the trip would not be found out when they compared our travel claims. I respectfully refused to perjure myself. All the Senior Chiefs were perturbed. I found myself being excluded from travel opportunities unless it was something I did alone.

Being a buddy with my supervisors who are the ones who have to face me at evaluation time was not one of the advantages I shared with a good number of my peers. But surprisingly to me, I got a great evaluation. The only problem was, all the Senior Chiefs in the office struggled over who was going to counsel me regarding my evaluation. They did not choose the most senior person, and they did not choose the Senior Chief who actually supervised me. They all got together and chose a really nice guy to give me reproof about their pet peeve.

Senior Chief (M.) sat me down in a quiet, otherwise unoccupied, classroom and filled me in on all the strong points that they liked about my performance. He explained that they were very pleased with my performance except in one area. "You talk about religion too much." I was thrilled for the admonishment. I was bracing myself for a report of some big character flaw that made me unworthy of my rank. Never-the-less, it was a criticism, and it was one which I felt would be perpetually held over my head and used against me. It seemed to me right away that the counseling session was an opportunity for them to document that I had been counseled regarding my "inappropriate" behavior. That was usually a prelude for being punished for the next occurrence.

I realized as I thought about it that the vast portion of my idle speech in the office was religious. Then I realized that I was nearly never the instigator of the conversations. In nearly all cases, I had been dutifully working at my desk when some lax busybody, who spent most of their working time in idle conversation, would interrupt my work with some sort of religious heckling. I rather shocked the Senior Chief with my reply.

"Senior Chief! You are right. I do spend a lot of time talking about religion in the office. I understand there is nothing wrong with talking about religion, only that it should not interfere with my work." (Senior Chief nods) "I appreciate you being honest with me and being willing to give me that kind of feedback." (Senior Chief has a satisfied look on his face). "However Senior Chief, I don't think its going to stop." (Senior Chief now has a shocked and angry look on his face.) "I guess you have not noticed that I am not the one who is starting religious conversations. And for the most part, I try to stay out of them. But there are certain people in the office who happen to spend the day reading the newspaper. They start all kinds of controversial conversations and interrupt me while I am working with a bunch of bogus questions in order to harass me." (Senior Chief nods and looks apologetic as he says he is going to also have a talk with [D.] as well) "Well, every time they ask me one of their questions, I try to think of an answer that has wisdom." (Senior Chief nods empathetically) "I just don't have it in me to give them an answer that is wise out of my own mind. So the only wise thing I can think of comes out of the Bible. And that is what I tell them." (Senior Chief has a blank, somewhat defeated look on his face) "And Senior Chief! I am taking what you say to heart and I am going to take it for action to make sure it does not interfere with my work. But when someone comes up to me and challenges me about my beliefs, I am going to answer them from the Bible." The Senior Chief just stared at me with his mouth open. After we stared at each other for a long awkward amount of time he said, "I wish I could do that."

Senior Chief (M.) went on to tell me that he had once been deeply religious and somewhat outspoken about his faith. He then confessed that he had given in to the temptation to join the crowd and fit in to the image that was expected of a sailor. It destroyed his zeal for the Lord and defeated him. I spent the next many minutes consoling the Senior Chief. I agreed with him that standing with Christ is a hard road but the internal consequences of capitulation were harder to bear than the loss of promotion possibilities. The Senior Chief had camouflaged himself. God gave me the opportunity to draw him out of the bushes. My willingness to stand fast to my Christ-First obligations did not bring me scorn; it opened up a door to minister to my superior.

As the two of us returned to the office, one of the hecklers shouted out my name and said, "What's with this latest thing about Jim and Tammy Baker?" I knew that all the supervisors were listening and they were aware I had just been told to not talk about religion. Senior Chief (M.) was only a pace behind me. So I did the Biblical thing. I said for all to hear, "I'm just going to worry about the beams in my own eye before I start worrying about the specks in somebody else's."

From that day forward, I saw a change in Senior Chief (M.). He often brought up conversations in front of the other Senior Chiefs about what his church was doing. The Senior Chiefs with him no longer tended to use brazen profanity and course jesting. We often had more conversations where I was able to encourage him in his faith. I was ultimately able to subtly disciple him in Christ without violating military protocol.

One of the biggest challenges to my walk of faith came upon my promotion to Chief Petty Officer in the summer of 1987. The infamous initiation came upon me. The Chief Petty Officer initiation is one of the great examples of hazing. It is where you are challenged to do things that are not necessarily dangerous, though often unhealthy. Many of the dares are certainly immoral.

The first day of the initiation, we (the initiates) attended an orientation meeting with all the Chief Petty Officers in our Division where we were given a list of do and don'ts for the following thirty days up to the frocking[17] ceremony on September 16th. We were required to get every Chief Petty Officer to autograph our "charge book". We had to assign a page for each person who would sign the book, and the pages had to be in the sequence of each person's rank and seniority. We were commanded to ask for their signature by quoting a standard line. It happened to include profanity and was very disrespectful. When the assignments were given, all in the room knew about my personal standards and they knew that I could not conform to their instructions without compromising my testimony. I asked the question, "What happens when we do not request the signature in just those words?" I expected to get a well-humored torture threat in the spirit of jest that the whole initiation was supposed to be about. What I received however was a sharp character assault. Besides being

---

[17] *Ceremony initiating all the promotees of that promotion cycle to the new rank prior to all of them being promoted in pay.*

denigrated by heart-felt profane insults, I was told that I either had to chose loyalty to the Chief Petty Officer fraternity or be permanently ostracized for the entirety of my remaining career. In so many other words, and possibly exactly those words, the heart-felt communication was, "We don't want people like you."

I had my initiation cut out for me, so to speak. I was not just an initiate, I was the enemy. I was a threat to their tradition. They thought I was heaven-bent on spoiling their revelry. Not participating was not an option. I had to find a way to be able to participate in the tradition without compromising my character in Christ. Soon after the first meeting, I was targeted by a Senior Chief in the office and given an assignment to deride the Command Master Chief with a few choice vulgar words. I was ordered to say every word verbatim and not tell him who gave me the assignment. It was very easy for me to determine that I would exclude the vulgarity. I wrongfully thought I could say the remainder of the statement thinking it was all part of the big joke. When I made the declaration about the Command Master Chief's competency, he was not amused. He asked me who told me to make the statement to him. I told him I was ordered not to say. He asked again who told me to make the statement. I assumed the proper humble posture and told him the Senior Chief's name. The Command Master Chief now had an order for me. "Tell Senior Chief (>>>) that I want him to come see me. Now!"

As I left the Command Master Chief's office, I realized how wrong I had been to be disrespectful even as an absurd joke. I realized that the nasty minded Senior Chief had gotten me to drop my Christian character guard on my first day of initiation. He got me to lose my witness for Christ with the Command Master Chief. I had begun to conform to the mold of the wrong potter. I stopped after about five steps out of the Command Master Chief's office and turned around to balance the record for my intended future success to retain my testimony for Christ. I entered his office and said, "Master Chief! I apologize for my disrespect. I should not let anybody influence me to do what is wrong. This initiation is no reason to change my standards regarding respect and protocol. I ask you to forgive me and I will not do it again." The Command Master Chief, true to his office, nodded with a look of empathy and said, "It's all right Petty Officer Carmichael. Just go tell the Senior Chief to come see me."

When I told the Senior Chief about his appointment with the Command Master Chief, my oppressor immediately began to try the

"Sergeant Carter in the face of Private Gomer Pyle" maneuver. I listened and said nothing. Just then, the telephone rang. It was the Command Master Chief wanting to know why the Senior Chief was not yet standing in front of him. When the telephone receiver had been taken off-the-hook, so had I.

From that point onward, I would act out an alternative that would give me an opportunity to demonstrate the character of Christ whenever I was assigned to do something that was contrary to it. For instance: When going to a Chief Petty Officer for him to sign my charge book, I would not say the standard blurb, "You are the ugliest %#$@*&% in the command and don't deserve to wear the uniform of a Chief Petty Officer. Go get me a cup of coffee and sign this charge book when you get back." I would instead say, "Chief Petty Officer so-and-so, I have the greatest respect for you as a Chief Petty Officer. I particularly admire the fact that you (a good character quality that was true about them). I will be honored if you sign my charge book. Could I get you a cup of coffee while you are signing it?" This was normally done in a public area and normally the observers would lash out at me with profane accusations about the motives of my behavior. Amazingly though, my complimentary comments would have a visibly positive affect on the Chief Petty Officer whom I was addressing. In all but one case that I can remember, the signatory would write an encouraging word that was a helpful hint about how to be successful in my new role. Every other initiate's charge book that I saw had many vulgar insults as well as gross things folded into the pages.

I was asked to do some things that were disgusting but were not immoral. If the disgusting act I was told to do was denigrating, I would decline the act and find an alternative keeping with the theme of the initiation. On the overnight hazing fun before the day of the frocking ceremony, we went through several hours of excruciating exercises dressed in our dungaree uniforms inside-out. We also got to eat strange things like live nightcrawlers, grubs and dog food (I opted for dog food). We enjoyed raw egg pop-sickles, many kinds of hot condiments, and other gross concoctions that we had no full idea of the contents. We were then transported to a ship where we got to enjoy the training program of the seagoing sort. Assignments were given to each initiate. Some were made to place frozen bait squid in their mouth. One man was given a live goldfish to hold in his teeth. They turned to me and ordered me to bite the goldfish in half while the other man held it in his teeth. I certainly would not enjoy biting a goldfish in half but it does not go to the point of immorality. However, getting my mouth close enough to the lips of the man bracing the tiny fish in order to carry out the order was totally against my, and the Navy's, moral code.

My fellow initiate winced at the concept of having our lips embrace while I bit the fish in half. Sadly though, as is typical of most initiates, he was too fearful to not concede to the overly humiliating impropriety. I heartily refused the order. I was immediately bombarded with exclamations of my initiators' enmity. It was not just a part of the initiation joke. They had counted me, by my actions, as unworthy of their fellowship. I was undaunted however since I had endured several weeks of their training program. I took charge. On the table in front of me, was a plate supporting a well-thawed whole squid. It had, no doubt, been in someone else's mouth several hours earlier. I abruptly and aggressively said to my antagonists, "Listen! I am not going to put my lips up against this man's mouth. That is totally inappropriate. I don't mind doing something gross, but I am not going to lower my moral and professional standards in order to participate in your silly game." I then grabbed the squishy squid, and squeezed the smelly thing into my mouth, having to press hard in order to get it all in. Then I began to chew. My audience began to groan in shocked disgusted pleasure. I continued to chew feeling the white saucy internal juices of the squid rush between my teeth. The immensity of the object overfilled my mouth cavity and incited a response from my gag reflex. I began to receive cheers from my fellow initiates as well as those torturers whose hearts were not set against me. As soon as I was able, though it took much longer than I had hoped, I swallowed the slimy cephalopod. I had earned a reprieve from immediate social exile.

The initiation experience was something that had a profound effect on my sturdy public stand for the things of God in my workplace. I came to understand that it is not about promotion. It is not about being a team player. It is not about fulfilling others' expectations of the traditional image of a cantankerous Chief Petty Officer. It is all about Lordship. Courage, tradition, and loyalty to the Navy mission, is what they are supposed to instill through their fraternal order indoctrination. However, by the actions of most of the leadership, submission of personal will and moral code to the will of the immoral majority is what they really induce. My antagonists should have relished the fact that their initiation program taught me to stand on principle and uphold Navy professionalism even in the face of such an onslaught.

I have no doubt that the Chief Petty Officer initiation is a point of decision in many people's lives. It manifests many childhood fears in the hearts of seemingly otherwise mature adults. It certainly manifested those fears in me: The fear of not being accepted; the fear of not being successful in my career in order to maintain my livelihood; the fear of public humiliation. If we have submitted our life to Jesus Christ, our decisions do not just hinge upon the consequences on our esteem or workplace competitive standing. They rest upon the old adage, "What Would Jesus Do?".

The day after I put on the khaki uniform, I had to deliver an immediate message to a commander who was in a meeting with the Commanding Officer. After I delivered the message, the commander asked me how I made Chief Petty Officer so fast (in seven years of service). With the Commanding Officer and other high ranking officers looking on, not having any wisdom of my own, of course I gave him the Biblical perspective. "Sir! Promotion comes neither from the East or the West or the South; but God is the judge. He sets one up and He puts down another."[18] I then respectfully left them in their stunned silence.

I learned through the initiation that acting by faith, according to the word of God, has powerful effects in all situations. It instilled in my heart a motto, "Always do that which is right rather than that which seems expedient." It gave me confidence to be about Christ and faith in every aspect of my life. As I look back now, it prepared me for a time of trial that, at the time, I would not have been able to imagine.

---

[18]   *Psalm 75:6-7*

Episode Five

The Perfect Irony

I had grown to thrill at the miraculous way Biblical principles affect Kingdom of God outcomes. The positive results of acting on God's word were so consistent as to be predictable. I began to realize more each day that there truly is a "Kingdom of God" at work perpetually.

The more I applied God's word for every situation, the more I saw His kingdom at work. The more I saw His kingdom at work, the more I desired to know about His kingdom, to see it come and the Lord's will be done on Earth as it is in heaven. I wanted the faith that Jesus called us to. I wanted to be able to believe God for all things. I wanted to see marvelous works like we read about others doing throughout the Holy Scriptures. I wanted to know what it was to hear the Father speak, and to do what the Father commanded. The major moment of God revealing Himself to me in that way came in the fall of 1987 during a visit to our church of a revivalist named Manley Beasley. One of the stories told by Brother Beasley made a significant impact on me. He recognized that our church congregational singing was pretty lively and he used our external "show" of zeal to prompt a poignant anecdote.

Brother Beasley had been invited to speak at a tent revival meeting. He pointed out that the congregation at this speaking engagement was extremely lively. Not only were they rolling down the aisles, they were shimmying up the tent poles. He gave a message on faith that really got the people excited. After he spoke, the church leadership ordered the taking up the offering according to the standard liturgy. Brother Beasley said the countenance of the congregation turned from one of celebration to one of a funeral. It upset him greatly and he strove with the Lord over it. As soon as the offering was taken up, Brother Beasley stood up and rebuked the congregation. He commenced to teach them about hilarious giving. He then ordered the ushers to come forward again to take up another offering where the congregation would now give a Holy offering to the Lord, by faith.

As the ushers were taking up the offering, the Lord began to challenge Brother Beasley about his own willingness to give <u>by faith</u>. The Lord pointed out to him that he had seven dollars in his pocket that he had not considered giving. Brother Beasley pointed out to the Lord that he needed that money to buy himself a shaving kit, since he had forgotten to pack one as he prepared for travel to the speaking engagement that day. He contended with the Lord that it would not be appropriate for him to come to the services with a budding beard. As he continued to contend with the Lord, he knew he would be in sin if he did not give his only seven dollars when the plates came forward to the altar. He grudgingly put the money in the plate and sat back down to await the close of the service.

After the service, a gentleman approached him and said "I don't know why, but before I came to the service, the Lord told me to bring this to you." What was it? Of course it was a shaving kit. The Lord used the situation to reprove Brother Beasley, keep him humble and remind him of the goodness and power of the Lord. The story gave me a glimpse of what it ought to be like to hear from God and obey his voice.

God used Manly Beasley's teaching on faith to introduce Himself to me in a way I had always hoped to experience. For the first time in my life I heard that faith had nothing to do with belief in the sense that we modern Americans normally consider. I learned that you can only act in faith when you actually <u>know</u> something to be true. You can believe something to be true even when you don't really know it to be true. You can <u>believe</u> something to be true that is actually false; but <u>knowledge of the absolute truth is necessary in order to act in faith</u>. Faith is acting on what you know to be true even if your sensory perception does not yet support the facts that you know.

There is an image that comes to my mind when I think about Moses at the Red Sea. Moses was a man of faith because he knew what was true in spite of what the situation indicated. Moses had with him over a million people who were operating in false belief rather than faith. Pharaoh decided to pursue them with his army and he converged upon them when they had the Red Sea at their back with no route of escape. The million plus Israelites <u>believed</u>, because of what they could see, that they were going to be killed by Pharaoh's army. Pharaoh and his army <u>believed</u> that they were going to do some killing. Their beliefs, though supported by empirical evidence, were based upon a falsehood. On the other hand, Moses <u>KNEW</u> the

Lord was going to save them. Fortunately, Moses acted on his faith rather what one might be led to believe. He called out to the people, "Do not be afraid. Stand still, and see the salvation of the Lord, which He will accomplish for you today. For the Egyptians whom you see today, you shall see again no more forever. The Lord will fight for you, and you shall hold your peace." Knowing the truth, he obeyed God and thrust his staff into the sea. His actions resulted in deliverance, making itself known physically. All the children of Israel were able to benefit as they hopped on Moses' faith bandwagon and entered the midst of the sea on dry ground.[19]

Throughout the week that Manley Beasley spoke to us, I was required to attend every service from Sunday night through Thursday night because I was part of the music team. God was really speaking to me through Brother Beasley each night of service. Brother Beasley pointed out walking by faith has a prerequisite; that you first know the will of God. It most often is already revealed in scripture. Sometimes however, God will give you a command to do something. Often times the word that God gives you will cost you something to obey. It may cost you your esteem, your pride, your job, your family, your friends

---

[19] *Exodus, chapter 14*

or seemingly your life. It may be a situation where by the Lord's leading, you place yourself in such a position that if God does not come through, you are sunk.

I desperately wanted to know what it was to truly live by faith in every aspect of my life. I knew the first night of this speaking engagement that I needed to get a word from God, that I would have to forsake all else to obey, in order for me to really know what it was to walk in faith. Every day and every night of Mr. Beasley's visit, I earnestly prayed to God that He would speak to me. I prayed in faith believing God would actually answer my prayer since I had no doubt that God wanted the same thing for me. Thursday had come, the last night of Mr. Beasley's visit, and I had not yet heard from the Lord. Mr. Beasley said there was no need for the music team on the last night of the conference. I was tempted to not go on that last night since it required us to drive thirty-four miles to church from our mobile home in Virginia Beach. I came to the conclusion that it would be a shame to have attended the other sessions and then miss out if God performed a mighty work on the last night. Mr. Beasley spoke the last night and his message did not make a big impact on me. He just seemed to summarize everything he had spoken through the week.

As he was closing in prayer and giving an invitation, my life was suddenly changed forever. God spoke.

During the invitation, I was a bit disappointed that God had not answered my prayer with an earth shattering revelation. I guessed I would have to keep praying and eventually God might see fit to speak to me when the time was right. My mind began to wander as my praying was not focused on any particular need. Suddenly, my thoughts were interrupted by a command that came to me. The reception did not come from the vibrating of my eardrums. It came into my mind displacing all thoughts in my head. I actually felt the presence of the Holy Spirit like the day of my salvation. The command came, "Sell your mobile home". I was shocked. I knew immediately that it was the voice of the Lord but I responded by praying, "Is that you Lord?". Again I heard, "Sell your mobile home". I was tempted again by doubt and I asked again, and suddenly I sensed a fearful disapproval in my spirit. I knew that to do anything else but sell our mobile home would be a grievous sin.

I acknowledged immediately, "Yes, that is you Lord. Thank you for your word. I will do it. I promise. Thank you for that word of faith." I turned to my wife sitting next to me and said, "God just spoke

to me. He said, 'Sell the mobile home'." My wife did not know what
to think. She had never heard me say anything like that before. She
just looked kind of surprised, shrugged her shoulders and turned back
to pray. I was so excited but I could not shout about it. There was
near silence as everyone was praying in response to the invitation. I
began to pray again as there did not seem anything better to do. I did
find myself embarrassed by my surprise that the Lord would actually
speak to me. I reminded myself that I earnestly prayed for it and
prayed believing He would do it. I was still amazed that He would
speak to me so suddenly, and just in time before the service was over.

The Pastor stood up to announce the conclusion of the conference
and he closed in prayer. He then walked pass me and I said "Brother
Leonard! I got a word from God. He told me to sell the mobile
home." With a somewhat impressed looked on his face, my Pastor
asked, "Then what are you going to do?" Suddenly, I was shocked
and slightly confused. There was a dilemma. I had no idea what to
do concerning the obvious fact that there were consequences to such
an action. I said, "I don't know, he didn't tell me that". His expression
turned to one of puzzlement.

Well! Now I could see the problem. God gave me a command

without telling me the full story of what must be done to take care of those practical physical needs that were a consequence of the task. I learned, by that first experience of getting a command from God, that a directive He gives me that requires me to carry it out by faith will most often have built-in problems. It requires me to trust in Him to intervene in order for me to survive or accomplish the mission. My wife was pregnant with our first baby and would have a physical and natural need to have the security of shelter. I had work to do. I had to spend a lot of time in prayer until God told me step two.

I immediately placed an ad in the newspaper. After doing the research to determine the selling terms, I found that the interest rates were lower for new mobile homes but higher for used mobile homes. It was cheaper for someone to purchase a brand new mobile home instead of buying our old one. Our newspaper ads seemed to be a waste of money. We were spending over $80.00 a month in advertising but nobody was calling us. Our mobile home was not necessarily situated in a prime spot for selling. We were under the final flight path of Oceana Naval Air Station. We could see the masked faces of pilots as they turned their jets just a few hundred feet over our heads. Double hearing protection was often warranted if we were out in the yard during flight operations.

People began to question my stability and spiritual maturity based upon my decision to sell the mobile home, at that particular time, and contrary to conventional wisdom. My mother-in-law was not too keen on the idea of me selling my wife's home out from under her at a time in her life when she needed extra security. During a Christmas family visit, my mother-in-law gave me good, wise, and seemingly godly counsel. "Wait until the baby comes to sell your mobile home. Give Les some time to get settled and give you some time to find a place to live. You don't want to be out on the street with a baby." I had never thought about the prospect of being homeless. That thought terrified me and I readily understood that I have a responsibility before the Lord to provide shelter and safety for my family. Scripture says, "…In a multitude of counselors there is safety."[20] It also says, "The way of a fool is right in his own eyes, but he who heeds counsel is wise."[21] It would be wrong for me to hear all this wise and godly counsel without heeding it. I did the "right" thing. I told my mother-in-law I would wait until after the baby was born to sell the mobile home.

---

[20] *Proverbs 24:6*
[21] *Proverbs 12:15*

This obedience to God stuff was becoming pretty complex. I guessed part of God's plan would be to steer my course through the counsel of other people.

After the vacation visiting my wife's family, my theories got rocked a bit. The first Sunday back home, the Pastor spoke about "standing on God's word", and specifically about the word the Lord gives you personally. Oh no! What was I going to tell my mother-in-law? I knew I had to tell my wife that I had to obey the command of God and just trust that He would take care of us. Because of unwarranted fear, I was not going to tell my mother-in-law anything until I absolutely had to.

Two months later I had the same problem but this time with my own mother. While visiting her in California, she urged me to not sell our home out from under my tender wife and soon-coming baby. I capitulated because my mother made such a sound appeal. I assured her I would wait until after the baby was born to sell our mobile home. I told her that having her and my mother-in-law give the same advice indicated to me that God might be giving me a reprieve on the mandate. To my dismay, the Sunday morning back at my home church subjected me to a morning Bible study of "Standing on God's

Word". The theme again was being obedient to a command of God specific to your situation. I knew that I needed to call my mother and retract my commitment to her. I did not know whether she would understand or not, but I needed to let her know I had sinned in making the promise to her. What I spoke to her in explaining my stance became known to me later as a confession of faith that God honored beyond that which I could dream.   It was the "Perfect Irony." I told her "Mom, God could sell (the mobile home) in ten years, He could sell it in two weeks, which would be great, or <u>He could sell it two weeks before the baby comes which would be the worst thing possible</u>. All I know, is that I have to sell the mobile home in obedience to God's word."

Time went on and we did not get any calls about the mobile home. I began to realize that the ad in the newspaper was doing nothing but wasting our money every month. I knew that there was really nothing I could do to make the mobile home sell. I retracted the newspaper ad and just put a "for sale" sign well situated in our front window.

One day while at church, a close friend of mine excitedly told me about a Veteran's Administration repossessed house that was for sale. He told me that it seemed to him and his wife that the Lord was prompting an excitement about it in their hearts and they did not understand why, since the price was more than he could qualify for on his single income. Sam described the house to us and it was a perfect description of the dream house my wife and I had outlined about a year before. It was a two-story, four-bedroom, two-and-a-half-bath, colonial. It was around the corner from our church, with a fireplace, room for dogs, room for a volleyball court, room for volleyball spectators, a front yard suitable for parking space, and it cost $77,500 at 9.5 % interest. The normal V.A. rate for mortgages at the time was 10.5% but this was lowered because it was repossessed. The features included all of those things we had listed as requirements, in our list of dream houses, even including the price and interest-rate which were in effect when we made the list. As soon as Sam told me about it, I got a prompting in my spirit that the Lord inspired them to look into it for our sakes. I said, "Sam, I don't want to spoil your plans or discourage you, but I think the Lord had you look into the house for us." We called a Realtor and scheduled a viewing. Sure enough Les and I believed the house was ours from the first moments we were on the property. The only problem was, we still owned a mobile home and had no prospects for selling it.

Episode Five

We obtained counsel from my pastor. He called one of our church members, Bruce Everheart, who is a real-estate agent. When Brother Leonard and Bruce understood our situation and the stirring God had placed on our heart about the house, we all came to the same conclusion. The right thing to do would be to place a bid on the house contingent upon the sale of our mobile home. Once the bid was in, we needed to sell the mobile home within a couple of weeks. A week went by and there was no one to sell it to. The V.A. received our bid and said they would need to know immediately when the mobile home was being sold. Bruce said the V.A. would consider the mobile home debt not a factor if we could get someone to make a one-year lease on it. The very next day, somebody telephoned and said they wanted to lease the mobile home for a year with an option to buy. I was extremely excited and believed they were the answer to ours prayers. The following day, the sermon again was about standing on God's word. My excitement about the prospect of being able to buy the home, on the basis of having secured a one-year lease, was quickly dispelled by my internal understanding that God wanted me to sell the mobile home, not lease it. I readily confessed my sin of being tempted to abandon God's plan because of my lust for the possibility of being able to purchase our dream home.

Within minutes of our getting home from church, the couple who wanted to lease the mobile home called and I had to tell them, "I'm sorry. God told me to sell the home, not lease it". The gentleman said words to me that indicated he thought I was an absolute kook. He did not attempt to argue with me. That day, my wife and I were a bit discouraged in one sense. Yet, we were encouraged by knowing that we had resisted temptation and had stayed obedient to God's command.

On Tuesday, the V. A. called and said we only had a few days to show we had a contract to sell the mobile home or they would reject our bid. Our hopes were dashed. We were broken-hearted. Leslie and I spent a couple of hours whining to one another about the predicament the Lord had put us in. We were frustrated and had many questions. Why would God tell us to do something that we were completely helpless to do? Why would He give us a prolonged mission that brought to us nothing but humiliation? Why would He allow us to get our hearts stirred up about purchasing the perfect home? When we looked back, it seemed that we had been stirred up about the house by the Holy Spirit, rather than by our flesh. We

Episode Five

oscillated between complaining and praying; from whining to praising. After all of the venting of our feelings, we came back to our senses and admitted that God loved us and had a plan that we just could not see. We were grateful for the spiritual growth we had experienced as our prayer time had intensified over the previous months. Though we were heart-broken, we resolved ourselves to the fact that the house we so desperately wanted may never be ours. God did not tell us to buy a house, He told us to sell our mobile home.

The next day, we were out doing yard work while the Navy jets were flying overhead on their landing approach to Oceana Naval Air Station. We noticed a gentleman coming up our walkway. We stopped our work to engage him in conversation. He asked how much we were selling our mobile home for. He had noticed the sign in our window as he was driving by looking for mobile homes that day. While I was answering him, we all had to stop our conversation, and cover our ears to protect our hearing, as an A-6 intruder flew by a couple hundred feet over our heads. Immediately I realized how unlikely the odds were for us to sell the mobile home situated as it was. Yet, he seemed undeterred in his interest about our mobile home and he began asking more detailed questions. So we showed

82

him all around, inside and out. He told us when he left that he was very interested. He thought the terms were reasonable but would have to think about it before he made his decision. I challenged him as to why he was still interested even after the jets flew over with deafening noise. He said it was no different from where he was living on the other side of the landing field. The next day he called and said he would buy the mobile home. By the Friday deadline, we were able to fax a copy of the mobile home sales contract to the V.A. Within a few days, the mobile home financing people arranged a closing date of Wednesday, May 11, 1988. Bruce called us and said the V.A. closing would be on Thursday, May 12, 1988. This was beyond remarkable. All this was arranged outside of our control. On Wednesday we sold the mobile home and on Thursday, only twenty days after submitting our bid, we purchased our house and were able to move in that day. God miraculously arranged a seamless transition from a tiny hovel to a comparative palace, just in the nick of time.

I shared the story with all my co-workers as I rushed around getting my leave request approved through the chain of command. I had to explain to them why, without any forewarning, I needed the time off to take care of personal business. As I told the story to my

Senior Chief, the whole Division was within earshot. One of the saltiest of the Senior Chiefs came to me after hearing the story and said to me under his breath, "I doubted all this God stuff, but after hearing that story, I am beginning to wonder."

But wait! There's more! I had nearly forgotten my words of faith. What did I say would be the worst thing that could happen? I said that selling the mobile home two weeks before the baby was born would be the worst possible scenario but I was willing to obey God none the less. And sure enough! Bethany was born Wednesday, May 25, 1988, a nice even fourteen days after the sale of the mobile home. I had another wonderful chance to tell everyone in my office about God's timing as I went through the chain of command with another request for leave so that I could be home to help my wife with our first baby.

Our Sovereign Lord had demonstrated His power and glorified Himself through our lives and our situation. God knows the web He weaves. I do not know if God has one plan that He forces us into, or if He has multiple plans, or if our acts of faith enable Him or cause Him to adjust His plans. Either way, I know I have the will to choose obedience or disobedience. Each choice will have differing results. It is something that I will never fully understand. It causes me to appreciate the mighty love and mercy our Father has for us yet at the same time causes me to have reverent fear for His justice. Through these events, I experienced first-hand that God does speak to us, we can hear Him, and obedience to His command has both eternal and temporal rewards.

Episode Six

Firewood & Cheetos

When we purchased the house, we stretched ourselves to our financial limit. Not that there was anything wrong with it. God knew our limit and He used it. Never-the-less, a couple of days after Bethany was born, I feared for our financial situation. We were out of cash and we still had some month left. My wife rebuked my irritability, telling me to calm down. She also exclaimed, "God did not bring us out of Egypt to die." She was right. Because of God's showing His power in our situation, we could never again get away with whining.

Since we got into the house on such a shoestring, we did not have the money to pay for the hook-up for Virginia Natural Gas. So I put that off until we needed it in the fall or winter. Since our house had a fireplace, and I as a city boy knowing nothing about firewood or chimney maintenance, I asked the guys in my office to give me some advice. They told me the type of wood that burned well, how long to let it dry after cutting it and what I had to know about taking care of my chimney. They told me that a cord of wood generally cost $100.00 or more.

I began checking a classified advertisement newspaper that was sitting in the office. I knew I did not have the money and sort of felt guilty that I was looking into such a venture knowing it would be extravagant to spend so much money for winter mood fires. Just then I heard the now familiar, rather than shocking, voice which said to the effect "I will provide you with firewood if you really need it."

After hearing the voice of God giving me the command to sell the mobile home, and after wrestling with the Lord over those many months that followed, I was readily able to recognize God's voice over my own thoughts. My first thought in response was, "Wow, that was God." I closed the newspaper and said words to the effect, "Okay Lord, if that's what you say, I'll just rest in that. Thank you." It sounds so far as if it was very easy. In actuality, it was very difficult. Of course it was easy to recognize the voice of the Lord. However, once I heard God, I had to make a decision. Was I going to believe Him at His word? Then, was I going to trust Him at His word? Since I had acknowledged to the Lord that He had spoken to me, I received the understanding that I needed to not take things into my own hands to provide for my need. This was a situation where God did not give me a command to obey, but instead He gave me understanding that my failure to rely upon Him, after His unsolicited promise to me, would be sin.

One of my Navy compatriots in the office, Dan, came to tell me of an opportunity where we both could get some wood at a very good price. I was in an office with about two dozen other men. After all my solicitations for help, I was a bit embarrassed that all of the sudden, unbeknown to them, I was now out of the cheap firewood search business. I tried to think of a way to dissuade Dan's zealous offers to get me in on a good deal without offending him and his gracious offer. I concluded that the best thing to do was to just tell him the truth. "Dan. Thanks for the offer but while I was reading this paper, God told me He was going to provide me with firewood. For

Free." Well, the office had six rows of people sitting at their desks and nearly every one of them heard my statement to Dan. They nearly in unison told me to "shut-up" and said "Yeah..Right! Get over it! Man, now I have heard it all!..." Anyway, I made sure I let them know that God really did speak to me.

This last little incident came and went without out much more fanfare. I mulled it over in my heart and mind for a few weeks but eventually forgot about it. What I find really fascinating, is the way that God worked an otherwise trivial event to spark my awareness of His word to me about the wood, and the need for me to obediently let Him do His work without letting my flesh interfere with it. God is really serious about what He says. And He really is paying attention to every detail, every thought, and every word.

Fall came upon us and I joined the command volleyball team. We played our games during lunchtime. One day, we had a tournament that took our games well beyond the normal hour. I wanted to do my best to sneak into my building and get back into uniform as soon as possible without anybody seeing me in my athletic attire during working hours. I entered through the back door of the building and hurriedly walked down the lonely passageway on my way to a rapid costume change. I did not have my contact lenses in, so my vision was just a little blurred. As I hurried down the hallway, I began to notice a bright orange object on the floor. I could not discern what it was. As I zoomed right over the orange object, it took me a couple more steps before I realized the object was a cheeto puffed corn chip. A few more steps later I considered that I ought to pick up that cheeto since it was right smack in the middle of the floor. I started to justify in my mind why it would be absurd to turn back around and pick up a silly cheeto, especially when someone else gets paid to clean up the floors later in the day. But then I came to the obvious conclusion that it was the right thing to do. All of a sudden, God spoke a scripture that I had recently become vaguely familiar with. "If a man knows the good he ought to do and does not do it, to him it is sin."[22] Oh man! Now I was under huge conviction of sin, over a cheeto. I immediately confessed it as sin of pride and laziness to the Lord. When you are late getting back to the office, you are walking around a military tactical training facility in your civilian exercise clothes and you are now about fifty paces away, spending the time to go back to get the cheeto at that moment did not seem to be keeping

---

[22] *James 4:17*

with propriety. I pleaded with God, "God, I will go back and pick up that cheeto. I promise. But I have to go get ready for work and back into my uniform. Then, I promise I will go back and pick it up. Lord? Could you remind me to pick it up in case I get distracted? Because I don't want to sin!"

So, committed to returning once I got into the uniform of the day, and trusting that God would certainly remind me to pick up the cheeto if I got distracted, I focused on getting ready for work again. Leave it to me though, by the time I was tying my last shoelace ready to leave the dressing room, I had completely forgotten about the cheeto. Suddenly, there was a loud noise behind me as a door slammed open. I turned to see one of my coworkers, Brian, out of breath and bedazzled looking. He exclaimed, "Chief Carmichael! There you are! I've been looking all over for you! I've got to tell you what happened to me. It's the most incredible thing I have ever experienced. I've been reading my Bible and I found a scripture I've never seen before. It's amazing. It has just changed my perspective about everything." Well this got me pretty excited and I had to calm him down to get him to just say what the scripture was. Can you guess what it was? Brian said, "It's James 4:17. If a man knows the good he ought to do and doesn't do it, to him it is sin."

Whew! How awesome is our God! He knows the thoughts and intents of our hearts so that He would use each of us to prove His power to one another. Brian was a guy who delved deeply into scripture to obtain the perfectly correct doctrine but he had no understanding of the things of the spirit. God used the instance to remind me He is speaking to us and leading us even in the most trivial aspects of our lives. I jumped up and told Brian what an awesome thing had just happened with God using him to fulfill my supplication of being reminded to pick up the cheeto. Brian was extremely perplexed when I told him that story.

While Brian and I were talking, our office scorner came out of one of the stalls and mocked me using a quote from Ben Franklin making a statement about "reason" that was completely out of context. Several things hit me at once. The first thing I thought; it was a good thing to have the scorner in earshot so he would be exposed to an uncensored testimony of the workings of God. The second thing was; I got frustrated because the scorner was such a bad egg that he could not help himself but mock us. The final thing was; I was fed up with the scorner being so irreverent.

That is when I really blew it. Trying to wield a bigger stick in the power of my flesh, I erred a much greater blunder than my antagonist did. I used the Bible to lash out at Him. I used the scripture completely contrary to its purposes and it's context. I said, "Yeah? And the fool does what is right in his own eyes."[23] I would have been better off just calling him a fool outrightly. It would still have been a great sin but not nearly so horrendous as the misuse of the Holy Scripture. Since the scorner made his comment while he was passing by, he was out the door by the time I got out the last word. I was grieved by what I had done. Rather than be able to enjoy the work God had done through Brian, I was in remorse over what I had done with my mouth. When I questioned to myself, "What shall I do?" I knew right away that I had to go apologize to the scorner.

So, that is what I did. I told Brian that I needed to be excused so that I could apologize to (M.). I hurriedly made the trip to the other side of the building in order to recover the cheeto. Instead of making the trip basking in the sense of victory that should come from knowing I was on a mission from God, so-to-speak, I felt like a chastened

---

[23] *Proverbs 12:15 "The way of a fool is right in his own eyes; but he who heeds counsel is wise."*

peon who reluctantly carries out his mandatory drudgeries. Having retrieved the squalid morsel, I tracked down (M.). I went right to groveling deeply once I found him. Surprisingly, I found that (M.) had not taken offense. He had actually been amused by my rude comment. Still, I forced him to hear to my apology. I needed to make it right before God.

After I had recovered from the trauma of failing miserably right after God manifested Himself in response to my prayer of faith, I went back into the office. The guys were talking about the precautions they were taking for the hard freeze that was coming that night. I asked them about the details of the weather forecast. They said it was going to be a record cold Columbus Day weekend with temperatures below freezing. It occurred to me too late that I still needed to get the gas hooked up for the furnace. A few men asked if I had gotten any firewood yet. They mocked me just enough to make it hurt when I told them I did not have any. Everyone was being let out early to get their houses prepared. I rushed home and telephoned Virginia Natural Gas to ask them if I could have gas supplied to my house for the weekend. They said someone would not be able to help me until Tuesday. They reminded me that I sure picked the wrong time to try to get my gas hooked up. So here I was with a new baby that was going to have to survive below-freezing temperatures with no heater in the house. It was nice to know we had a fireplace but we did not have any firewood. Now I woefully remembered that God told me He would provide me with firewood and I was a little disappointed that we really needed it right then and He had not come through for me. I needed a miracle but, after my infidelity regarding the misuse of God's word that day, I certainly did not feel that I warranted any special blessing from God.

Leslie asked me what we were going to do for firewood. She asked if we were going to have to survive off of firewood from the local Seven-Eleven mini-mart. She said that we needed to get there pretty quickly before they sell out. I don't know whether I had told her that God said He was going to provide the wood or whether she had just forgotten about it. I knew very well that God had impressed upon me that I was supposed to trust Him for it. But, we had a need, and here was my wife giving the logical solution. I would seem extremely irresponsible, and in the words of (M.) - without reason, if I told my wife we were not supposed to buy any wood because God told me that He would provide it for me at no cost. Because of the potential humiliation, I did not bring up the subject. There was one thing for certain that made us both aware that we needed to trust God. We had less than twenty dollars and knew the Seven-Eleven option was not going to save us. I tried to stall Leslie and distract her from the Seven-Eleven idea, hoping I might be able to either search for, or stumble across, some firewood left as refuse somewhere in or near some woods. I said, "We don't even have one of those metal things you put the logs on (andiron). We looked in a Builder's Square magazine that had come in the mail. Fortunately, andirons were on sale that day or we would not have been able to afford one. It fit right into my distraction scheme and depleted our money enough to not even be able to afford a set of fire-logs. I said, "Why don't we just go to Builder's Square and buy one of those things and then we can worry about getting wood on the way home."

I still had not learned about the salvation of the Lord yet. God is faithful even when we have no faith. Just as we were leaving the house, knowing I did not have the guts to really believe God for the firewood, the phone rang. My wife was already going out the door with the baby and I was right behind her. I was tempted to let the phone ring since daylight was wasting, but I felt what is often called a "check" in my spirit. I felt (like a premonition) that I ought to answer the phone. I stopped my wife at the front door and I stepped back into the kitchen to answer the phone. It was my Pastor and here I quote him. "Hello brother, would you like some firewood?"

Yes it is true. Right in the nick of time. Wow! I was excited, I was embarrassed, I was grateful and I was penitent in my heart. God had spoken to me. God had fulfilled His promise. He did not do it ahead of time, He did it right on time. The only thing that I did by faith was to acknowledge to God that I had heard Him speak to me. I was embarrassed that when push came to shove, though I vowed in my heart that I would not intervene to meet my own need, I was readily tempted to take things into my own hands.

My Pastor had recently changed his conventional fireplace to a gas fireplace. While I was internally struggling with the temptation to solve my own problem contrary to my vow to trust God for that specific provision, Brother Leonard was standing in his backyard and coming to the conclusion that he wanted to be rid of his obsolete logs immediately. He thought to himself, "Who do I know that has a pick-up truck?" He thought of me as well as others but I was the one who lived closest to him. I left my wife to wait at the house while I loaded up my pick-up truck with enough logs to last a season. We then made our trip to the store to buy fireplace equipment and had a marvelous time worshiping our Lord as we basked in the warmth of the hearth and successfully heated the whole house by convection.

Episode Seven

Visions and Dreams

Does God speak to people like He did in the Bible? Some say that God does not speak to people today and some say He does. Some claim to have first-hand knowledge of God speaking. Others however, I suppose, have first-hand knowledge of God <u>not</u> speaking. I know it is very important for me to measure every spiritual experience with the appropriate Biblical context. I have to make sure what I am experiencing is truly from the Lord and not from my vain imagination or demonic influence. At the same time, I have to be willing to truly trust God, just as Jesus showed us. Jesus told us to have faith like little children. I believe He was serious about what He said.

I read in scripture that those who hear God's voice come to Christ.[24] Faith comes by hearing, and hearing by the word of God.[25] Even the reading of scripture does not give understanding by the mind but by the spirit of God.[26]

At one time, I had not known the experience of God speaking directly to me. By what I could see in the scriptures, God has every intention of speaking to His children. So, by faith (since the scriptures are the word of God) I believed (in the true sense) that God does speak to His children.

Sometimes a word from God comes to me as a specific directive that I can quote. Just like when Jesus spoke to Saul of Tarsus. "Saul, Saul. Why are you persecuting me? ...I am Jesus, whom you are persecuting. It is hard for you to kick against the goads."[27] Not only does God speak to me in words that I can directly quote, He gives me understanding of the broader meaning beyond the direct quote. It is like when the Apostle Peter was given the vision of "unclean" animals coming down out of heaven. He was also given the direct statement

---

[24] *John 6:45*
[25] *Romans 10:17*
[26] *John 3:3-6; 4:23-24; 6:60-64; 16:5-15*
[27] *Acts 9:4-5*

that he could quote, "What God has made clean, you must not call common." When he obeyed the command of God, Peter obtained a broader understanding of God's intention to redeem all of mankind, and not just the Jews.[28]

I had a few experiences like that. I once had a dream where I saw and spoke with the Lord Jesus. During the dream, I deeply sensed the presence of the Lord in my spirit. I was in a crowded room filled with people from my church that were just mingling about and socializing with one another. It was what we call "having a fellowship". They were all having a very good time and there was a high volume of sound from their joyful banter. Suddenly, I experienced the awesome fear that comes from being in the presence of the Lord. By reflex, I fell to my face. I experienced the conviction of sin mingled with the forgiveness and love of God. Then I became aware that Jesus was standing in the middle of the room just a few feet away from me. I became even more reverent. I was awed and thrilled that "He" had come and visited us in person. I noticed that the banter in the room continued. I was ashamed of their total disregard of the physical presence of Jesus. Then understanding crept upon me.

---

[28] *Acts 10 - specifically verse 15 (HCSB)*

They had no idea that He was there. I, on the other hand, was certain that He truly was there. He was not just an abstract vision. In silent prayer, I questioned to myself and to the Lord about why the others were not aware of His presence. Then the Lord told me. "Mind not the physical, but the metaphysical." Along with that quotable direct statement, He gave me understanding. I understood that His presence, His kingdom, the kingdom of heaven, His realm, is more "real" and more "physical" than all the things around me that I can see, hear, touch, smell, and taste. I had never heard the word "metaphysical" before but the Lord gave me the full understanding of it's meaning when He spoke to me. I understood "metaphysical" to mean: "The other physical", wherefore the spiritual realm is just as tangible, and physical, and real, and present, as those things that are readily detectable by our senses. I understood it better than I can put into words. I understood it better than Webster's Dictionary could put into words.

When I woke up, I still had a powerful sense of the presence of the Lord. I kept mulling over the particular words of the Lord Jesus. "Mind not the physical, but the metaphysical." I kept questioning to myself whether He actually used the word "metaphysical" because at that time I had not been exposed to that word. I thought that God had sort of made up a word that made sense to me by the context of the situation. Then I thought to myself, "Why would God give me a specific "WORD" that was not really a word?" I concluded, almost disgusted with myself, that it had to be a real word and that I ought to be able to find it in the dictionary. Of course, there it was.

I got a sense of understanding from the Lord that His message was specifically for me, my situation, and my situations to come. I knew in my spirit that it was not a word for His body (though the rest of the church could use it), it was a word for me. "For him who has ears to hear." I am not saying that God's specific word to me was a command to delve into metaphysics, as many today would define it. God's word to me was not a command to enter into divination. I understood that His word to me was a powerful and urgent admonishment to seek first His kingdom and His righteousness. God wanted me to train my thoughts toward His will and purposes for my life; to trust Him greater than I trusted those things that I could see.

So far, some of the "words" I received from the Lord may seem pretty innocuous compared to those words received by many in the Bible. The "Sell the mobile home" command was actually pretty significant. It really required me to act on faith. It was a word that I had to obey even though there was great risk of obedience making us homeless. It went against what many other people thought as responsible behavior. The firewood and cheeto "words" may seem almost frivolous. Yet, they were convincing works of God to spur me on to seek His face, to hear His voice, to obey His word without hypocrisy, and to trust Him for the smallest detail of my need. As a result, my faith grew even more rapidly.

I was eventually transferred from shore duty to sea duty. In the fall of 1992, on-board the USS THOMAS C. HART, I was in a fairly comfortable spiritual state. I was continually examining the Lord's will for my future. I understood early on in my Christian life, that God intended for me to be in some full-time Christian ministry. I began to pray asking the Lord what I should do to prepare for His plans.

My ship went to sea for seven weeks in October and November of 1992. Some very interesting things began to happen during that time. The lines were cast off the pier, the tugs pulled the ship outside of the slip, we cast off the tug lines, we secured the sea and anchor detail, and I began to return to the skin of the ship. All of the sudden, I got a word from the Lord. It was as if I was being rebuked. The

Lord said, "Refinance your mortgage for a 15 year loan." His word came with a sense of impending doom. With the "word" came the understanding that I was not supposed to fiddle around with the idea. I had to act on it immediately and just trust God to work it out for my best interest (natural pun not necessarily intended). I stopped in my tracks and responded to Lord as if I was pleading for relief, "Okay Lord! I will apply to refinance the loan the first day back. I won't even check the rates." Suddenly, I felt a sense of relief, as if I was no longer in trouble. I understood that the Lord was very serious and I was not to take my oath lightly.

As that underway time continued, I was in a steady state of prayer. I prayed, "What should I do to prepare for my future ministry?" I weighed the consequences of the preparations required. My underway schedule was very busy and I had to set apart time to spend with my family. If I took college courses, it would cost even more time. I understood that a sacrifice has to be made if you want to accomplish something that's worthwhile. But it would have to be a mandate from the Lord for me to do anything that cost time spent with my family. As I prayed, the Lord gave me the understanding that He did not want me to spend my time trying to get some kind of college degree. But as I got a reply from a Lord, I was confused. So I began to ask, "Lord? How am I going to be qualified to do anything in ministry when I get out of the Navy?" At that time, I believed that I had no qualifications to do anything except be an electronics technician. I presumed the Lord would have me in the Navy until the completion of a twenty-year career. I would have retirement money to subsidize whatever ministry I was assigned. As I was diligently seeking an answer from Lord, He gave one. He said, "You do not need accreditation. I am your accreditation." With those words came the understanding of His will in my situation. Taking college courses at that time would be chasing the wind. It would be my efforts to accomplish what I think would be a good thing on its face to do for the Lord's service.

God normally gives me a specific word so that I know exactly what I am supposed to do or not to do. He also gives me a sense of what is right to do, or not to do, regarding things that might somehow affect His overall plan relating to the "word" He has given. Beyond the word that I could not pursue accreditation, I understood that educating myself was not wrong. It was just not something that I was supposed to be devoting all my resources to.

When I got the word from the Lord and understood Him, I did what is always natural, I opened my mouth and whined asking another question for clarification. "What am I supposed to do between now and retirement? I feel I need to do something so I won't look back and think I wasted time." The Lord reproved me immediately. He said, "If you want something to work on, work on your music." With each word I get from the Lord, I am always amazed. He actually speaks to me in conversation. I understood immediately again, that what I heard was a specific "word" from the Lord. He was going to be my accreditation for whatever ministry that He had prepared for me. Also, working on my music abilities would not be chasing the wind. He did not give me a specific word about how I would use it, He just gave me a peace that working on music would be productive.

Very troubling though, I sensed from the Holy Spirit that we were going to be <u>poor</u>. Whatever God had intended for my ministry future, it would mean that we would have humble means for survival. The Holy Spirit did not give me a sense of doom; He gave me a sense of soberness. When I sensed that He intended for us to be in a state of poverty for some time, I pleaded with the Lord, "Please talk to my wife! I don't know how I'm going to explain all of this to her." God is more than faithful. I had no idea how strong God would show Himself in response to our short conversation.

The remainder of the seven-week period underway was fairly uneventful. For the most part, I just kept the words that God gave me in the back my mind. I did spend some time talking to the Lord, continuing to seek His assurances. I kept asking Him to speak to my wife to prepare her for future ministry that may include some financial discomfort.

The day I got back from sea, Leslie met me on the pier with our children and our friends, Sam and Beth, and their children. Sam and Beth were staying at our house for a few days. We visited with them until well after midnight. We were all very exhausted and went to bed. I'd been aware all night that I was supposed to tell Leslie about the words that God gave me. I learned up to this point that when God speaks to me, it is very important to confess what He has spoken. It makes me accountable to my fellow man to ensure that I'll carry out what God has commanded. We got into bed and had some end of the day small-talk. I kept the conversation going a bit awkwardly. I tried work up the courage to break the news to Leslie about the directives I got from the Lord.

As I lay in bed, I struggled in a silent state of prayer. I was wrestling with my conscience. Since Leslie was exhausted, I hesitated to bring up such an intense conversation before she went to sleep. The conversation subsided and I had still not brought up the subject. Leslie appeared to drop off to sleep. It would be a rather cruel thing to wake her at two in the morning. I told myself that the reasonable thing was to just bring it up in the morning when we both woke up. Just like you are not supposed to let the sun go down on your wrath, you should also not let the sun go down on your word from the Lord. I knew in my heart that I would put off telling her, potentially indefinitely, if I did not rouse her.

Unbeknown to me, Leslie was struggling herself. She appeared to be trying to get to sleep as fast as she could. Internally however, she was stressed more than I was. She had something I needed to hear and she was having the same debate within herself that was going on within me. Suddenly, I was aroused from my internal debate with unexpected words from Leslie. "David? I have something I need tell you." The intensity of her voice alerted me that what she had to say was extremely important, even urgent. She began to apologize. She said words to the effect, "I know you're in charge of the finances and I don't want to intrude upon those things that are your responsibility. I don't want you to get upset with what I am going to say. But while you were gone, the Lord impressed upon me that it is very important for us to pay off the house as soon as possible."

As she continued to speak, I tried to interrupt her. A mighty miracle had happened and she did not know about it. I tried to tell her that God had given me the same word. But instead of hearing what I was saying and being excited about it, she was irritated. What God had impressed upon her was so strong that she badly needed to be able to share it with me. Everything else paled in comparison. She shut down my interruptions and told me she had something else to say. I kept my mouth shut to give her an opportunity to speak. I realized that eventually I would have a chance to tell my exciting part of the story.

Then, another mighty miracle of God occurred. Leslie said that God had showed her that we would one day be involved in a music ministry. I was thrilled by her revelation that was akin to mine. I tried to tell her my half of the story so she would know that God had performed a miracle. I knew that the revelation she received was more significant than she could yet have imagined. But to my chagrin,

God had impressed the whole thing upon her so strongly that she did not care what I had to say. There was nothing I could say to make His "word" to her more significant. She had to work hard at it but she kept me silent while she told me her understanding of God's will for us. I became in awe as Leslie manifested the answer to my very earnest prayers. God no doubt had an important plan for us. He was not only speaking to me, He was speaking to my wife. He was listening as well. God answered my prayer. He prepared my wife for His plans that I sensed would bring us to meager means.

The next business day, Monday, I telephoned our mortgage company to schedule an appointment to refinance the mortgage for a fifteen-year loan "as soon as possible". They had a waiting list that was stacked up many weeks. There was an appointment that had just been canceled. If I could get there in the allotted time (fifteen minutes) with the appropriate amount of cash, they would let me apply. We grabbed our shoes, and our cash envelopes, and we rushed out the door. Our interest rate was lowered two-and-a-half percent. Our payments were essentially the same but we cut ten years off the loan. Very soon thereafter, my Mother purchased a digital piano with weighted touch sensitive keys for me to work on my music.

Episode Seven

Time went by fairly uneventfully for a while. We got caught up in the distractions of day to day living. Though we were deeply involved in various ministries at our church, things kind of became routine. One day, Leslie and I were visiting with people in the vestibule adjacent to the sanctuary at church. A lady, Renee, came up to us and gathered the both of us together away from our separate distractions. She began to tell us that the previous night, she had a dream that she believed was from God. In the dream, Leslie and I were on a platform or stage of some type, leading young adults or older teens in worship music. Renee apologetically said that she felt God had impressed upon her that she needed to tell us about the dream. Her vision sparked us out of our doldrums. We were enthused by Renee's vision. We encouraged her by telling her the story about God giving Both Leslie and I the same word. Just like when Leslie got the word from the Lord, Renee was not too impressed by what we said. She was already overwhelmed by the sense of God speaking to her.

Then time pressed on again. God reminded us, through Renee's vision, that He had an important plan. But as usual, we fell back into spiritual doldrums rather that pursuing a special work of God. One evening, I received a telephone call from a friend who wanted to come over and visit. We soon heard a knock at the front door. We opened it to see the entire Leon Everett family standing on our stoop. They seemed to be preoccupied with some concern, based upon the looks upon their faces. They had a look like they were coming over to tell me I had offended them and they need to clear up the problem. Leon had a guitar with him. It made me then wonder if Leon wanted me to show him a particular guitar playing technique, or a song. Maybe they just wanted to have an impromptu praise and worship sing-along.

After they all sat down, Leon said his wife Cindy had something she needed to tell me. Cindy told me that God had given her instructions to come tell me about her dream. Firstly, she told me that she had entered a raffle at a music store and ended up winning a guitar. Then very recently, God gave her a dream where she saw Leslie and I leading people, young adults in their twenties, in worship music. When she woke up, she felt the presence of the Holy Spirit very strongly. The Lord showed her that she needed to give me her guitar and to tell me about her dream. Cindy told me recently that it was actually a vision and not a dream because it was so real to her.

Episode Seven

The Lord gave her an intense sense of urgency that she needed to get the guitar to me and tell me about the vision as soon as she could. She had a deep faith struggle through it all. She presumed I would think she was being absurd. However, she also sensed that she did not have the option of not doing what God commanded.

Leslie and I were quite sobered. We had nearly forgotten both the word God had given us and the vision that he gave Renee. Again, we had let our spiritual pursuit lapse into complacency. Leslie and I got very weepy-eyed. We looked at each other and shook our heads in silent agreement of our need to repent and earnestly pursue the Lord. We pulled ourselves together and explained the whole story to the Everetts. After affirming them with our story, we accepted the guitar as a very special gift from the Lord. We vowed to not forget the word God gave to us, or the visions He gave to others for us.

God gave Leslie and me an assurance of His plans for us rather than a call to seek out a music ministry. God told me that He would be my accreditation for the ministry He planned for me. The Holy Spirit also made me understand that we would be poor. He was beginning to prepare us for a much larger scheme than just music ministry. Cindy's very valuable gift to me was actually a gift to the

Lord for His work. It was a precursor to many hundred events like it in the days to come. God had begun to give us a hint of His purpose and His power. I liken it to a subtle rumble of thunder from a storm in the distance on a summer afternoon. You cannot see the storm clouds through the bright sunshine and hot summer haze. Yet, when you hear a rumble, you know something is on the approach.

Episode Eight

Loving Not My Life

Telling someone that God literally spoke to you is a very risky thing. Most people will think that you are having delusions. Even those who believe God speaks will generally consider your statement with great skepticism, rightfully so. Whether or not God has actually spoken to you will be seen over time. Once God has spoken to you, and people have seen His work associated with it, folks will at least entertain the idea the next time you tell them God has spoken. Whether or not you adhere to the path that God gives you when He speaks cannot rest with how well it is taken by others around you. The Bible is full of instances where the religious 'right' incorrectly concluded that their prophets were 'wrong'.

In my life, the key has been recognizing the difference between God's voice and my own thoughts. I have heard the Lord, obeyed His directives, and seen the resulting miracles. He confirmed His work often enough for me to be able to associate the difference between a word of His and a thought of mine. In every case prior to 1995, I experienced relatively rapid confirmation of His speaking. The mobile home sale took about six months. The firewood took about three months. The cheeto took about twenty minutes. The word about music and paying down our mortgage was confirmed within hours of my returning home from sea. There were many other instances not included in this book. Suffice to say, I recognized the voice of God when He spoke to me in the person of the Holy Spirit.

Up to that point, God was speaking things that were ultimately good news for us. There came a time, beginning in the fall of 1994, when God began to whisper things that were not good news for me. His words were very troubling. They were things that I did not want to hear which gave me thoughts I did not want to entertain. If I told you what the Holy Spirit told me, you would be troubled to. Thus, I have tried to write this chapter several times before coming to this approach. I do not want my reader to be troubled, I want the reader to be hopeful. Nothing I should say should trouble you. God is faithful to tell you troubling things if that is what He wants you to hear. I read that the Holy Spirit told Paul directly, and by prophetic words through others, that he was going to be taken from Jerusalem in chains and be delivered to the Gentiles. It was ominous, but ultimately good news for the entire world. God used Paul's imprisonment as a mighty tool to further the Gospel throughout the world, as it is still being used today.

Here, I rephrase the opening question in this book: What would you do if God spoke to you, and it was something you did not want to hear? What if God gave you a task that was something you did not want to do? What if it was something that nobody else wanted you to do?

For instance, what if, like Fred Snider in Episode Two, God told you to quit your job and move to a city a hundred miles away from your friends and family, without telling you why you were going?

Think about what you would have to deal with. The first thought is fear for your survival. It is risky quitting a job without having another one waiting for you. Secondly, your wife depends upon you. Not only for provision, she depends upon you being mentally and spiritually stable and trustworthy. Would you go to her with a statement like this? "Honey! I have some good news and some bad news. First the good news. God spoke to me today."

"Now the bad news. He wants me to throw away our livelihood; abandon our friends and family; give up our home; appear to everyone around us like we are nuts; go to a new place where we do not know anyone; we will have no physical means to recover the things we are losing; and He is not telling us what good, if any, will come out of it."

Would your wife say in response, "Oh Honey! I am so excited! I can't wait to see the results of your obedience!" For most of us, the result might be just the opposite. "You have got to be out of your mind! I hope you don't expect me to sacrifice everything to play along with your silly whim!"

Now if God told your wife the same thing that He told you, she would probably look forward to the exciting adventure. God does not always make it easy for us by clueing our spouse in on His plan. Sometimes, God asks us to do things that are extremely difficult, and costly. In my case, God asked me to change my dependency.

In 1995, I was presented with the opportunity to apply for early retirement. That career option was something I had never contemplated. Since I considered my career to be subject to God's bidding, I prayed about it. I felt a firm assurance in my spirit that God did not want me to apply for early retirement. Alarmingly though, the Holy Spirit gave me no assurance that my career would continue to its normal end at twenty years where I could qualify for retirement. In fact, I got a sneaking suspicion that I was not going to make it that far. I was perplexed and slightly troubled.

Not too long afterward, I began to hear the Lord speak in a still small voice. I am deliberately very cryptic about what God told me. How do I fully and accurately explain a concept that even the Bible conveys as a mystery? I have no desire to convince everyone to jump on my theological bandwagon. My intention is to emphasize the cost of discipleship.

Let me give you a hypothetical example. Let's say God spoke to you and told you that the Social Security Number was the Number of the Beast (NOB). Your first reaction would probably be rejection of the word. You have had superb and well-accredited teaching on the subject. First of all, the NOB will not manifest itself in your lifetime, or at least not until after you are taken into heaven. Secondly, it will come along with a challenge to deny Christ. Thirdly, the NOB is some sort of tattoo. Fourthly, any word spoken by the Lord would not conflict with well-founded Christian dogma. Lastly, participation with the Social Security Number is required by law. We are admonished in scripture to submit to every ordinance of man..."[29] You would have to live in America without being able to work, vote, drive, bank, bear arms, or do any licensed activity. You would live in America as if you were an enemy of the government and its people. It would cause you to put yourself in conflict with Caesar, bringing shame to the name of Christ. All of those thoughts would be very rational and responsible for someone who has been well reared in the modern church. You would certainly consider that you would damage your testimony if you went off on such a limb.

A similar thing happened to me. God was giving me an understanding of scripture that was not the popular interpretation. The literal application of the scripture, that He gave me to understand, would place a boundary upon my life that other people would consider extravagant and unbiblical. It was really not unbiblical but it was certainly unconventional. It went against the popular dogma but it is something that is admittedly a mystery. Many have resigned

---

[29] *1 Peter 2:13*

themselves to a "wait and see" attitude in their opinion on the subject. One of the major problems for me was, if I obeyed God, I would come in conflict with a standard practice of my employer, the United States Navy. I would have to disobey God until I could sneak out of the Navy, or I would have to ask for a religious accommodation. Asking for a religious accommodation makes people think that you are not loyal to your country. I was about to get transferred to my last shore duty before a twenty-year retirement. I would have wasted an arduous seventeen-year investment. It would affect my not being able to be hired in the future. I would lose credibility for my hopes of getting involved in a Christian ministry position after the Navy. Worst yet, people would scorn me for throwing away my career and retirement for something that most Christians believe the Bible does not require.

But, what if the voice you heard seemed to sound just like the voice of God that you have been listening to for years? What if that voice came accompanied by a deep sense of the moving of the Holy Spirit? What if it came along with a understanding of God's plan regarding the whole thing, as well as an understanding of the subtle paradoxes of scripture? What if it came along with the understanding that God wanted you to be obedient even at the cost of your livelihood, reputation, ministry, and friends?

The understanding that God gave me about many popular scriptures that are taken very lightly, shined light on my allegiance to Him. I discovered that I did not completely trust God's word enough to act on it literally. My dilemma was that taking God at His word literally would mean that I would have to give up the life that I knew. There are certain things in scripture, if taken literally, will conflict with the typical daily requirements of livelihood. Not only that, if acted out literally, it will cause other Christians in this American culture to consider you as a heretical fanatic. Again, what those particular literal things are is not my point here. What is important is whether or not we are really willing to put God's word into practical application in every aspect of our lives.

My knee-jerk reactions to what God was putting into my heart were very natural, rational and to be expected. My flesh and earthly rationale were warring against God's call for me to completely live by faith. I cried out to God in a way that would essentially be just short of blasphemy. If I could have plugged my fingers into my spiritual ears in order not to hear Him, I would have done so. I complained to the

Lord that conforming my life to His word, both spoken and written, would be overly costly. I had a family to think about who needed to have food on their table, as well as clothing and shelter to survive. They also had a need to belong in Christian society and not be ostracized as family members of a lunatic father. Our extended family would not look well upon me putting my family at risk for something they did not, or could not, understand.

I had invested many years in a Navy career and had expected to be able to use a Navy retirement/retainer pay to subsidize a ministry. Besides all of that, I just could not bring myself to risk everything for the sake of the prompting of a "still small voice." I told the Lord, "I have my children to think of". When I used that excuse, God spoke to me very directly and clearly. "If you cannot stand now, how will they stand later?" That word cut deep into my heart, mind and soul as the Holy Spirit convicted me.

As far as using the retirement pay to subsidize a ministry, Jesus did not call people into ministry if they had a financial buffer. He called them to completely trust Him for those things necessary for daily life. I knew that God wanted me to yield to Him completely; to obey His word literally; even though nobody else seemed to be taking the same path. The Holy Spirit gave me the sense that He would, again, bring about the perfect irony. Though it seemed that obedience to God would bring about the worst ramifications possible, the actual net result would bring about blessings unfathomable.

My acting out God's word in each area of my life would cause conflict with Navy procedures. This conflict with the Navy's way of doing business would require one of two things. I would either have to let my enlistment lapse and then obey God or I would have to obey God and ask for a religious accommodation. In the second option, If the Navy did not take my request seriously: I could get kicked out; I could get punished; I would bring shame upon myself and my family; I would be ridiculed and scorned; and I would face other problems that I could not imagine. In the first option, I might be out of a job but I could save face. I could try to make people believe that I was getting out of the Navy for a noble cause. The real problem with that first option is that God did not call me out of the Navy; He told me to obey His word. Also, I would have to be denying God's mandates for me while my career continued up to the end of my enlistment. I would be committing a grievous sin. My exit from the Navy would save some public shame but God and I would be very aware that it would be an act of disobedience.

I began to have Gethsemane like prayer times. In the Navy they use a term "sweating bullets." I writhed, moaned, and complained to the Lord, asking Him to cut me some slack. I pleaded with Him to just let me bide my time and wait to get out of the Navy quietly. However, I seemed to get no peace. With each day that I put off what I knew was inevitable, I became more and more conscious of my sin. It was a sin that was ultimately one of denying Him. When I did not get a reprieve with the typical prayer posture, I went to fasting. Still, I got no relief. The only thing that the intense prayer did was to confirm in my heart that God was calling me to sell out to Him completely. It was His way or the highway.[30]

With Jonah, God caused a great storm to come upon him to turn him around from running away from God's assignment. With me, God gave me a word.

One early morning at sea, during battlegroup exercises, I got up to go on watch. I had relieved the watch a little late the day before and I

---

[30] *"Enter by the narrow gate; for wide is the gate and broad is the way that leads to destruction, and there are many who go in by it. Because narrow is the gate and difficult is the way that leads to life, and there are few who find it." Matthew 7:13-14*

wanted to get there plenty early this time. I wanted the new guy, whom I followed in the watch rotation, to know that I was not in the habit of relieving people late. I finished getting dressed and ready for the day about 5:15 a.m. I made up my bunk in the dark, and I turned to head up to CIC.[31] Suddenly, I got this command from the Lord to read my "Days of Praise" devotional booklet.[32] It was definitely a strong command of God and not a thought of my mind. I actually only read the booklet a couple of times a week when it was convenient. This was not convenient. I was in a hurry. I started rationalizing why I should not stop to get the booklet and read it. Then I was stricken by an ominous sense of urgency impressed upon me by the Holy Spirit. My Earthy tendency again argued; (this time not to myself but to the Lord) "Lord! I've got to relieve the watch. If I read the thing, I won't have time to meditate on it. So what's the use?" I thought about just taking it with me. I realized it is not appropriate to stand around reading my religious devotional in the middle of a major battle problem. So, I started to resume my trek out of the berthing compartment and the Lord spoke strongly to me again. "Read it!"

---

[31] *Combat Information Center.*
[32] *Institute for Creation Research (ICR) publication.*

Like a frustrated teenager, I groaned and reluctantly returned to my bunk, grabbed a pipe on the overhead and lifted myself up into the bed. I turned on the small light, reached into my bunk bag and pulled out the "Days of Praise." I opened it to August 13, 1996. It said:

"Do not think in your heart that you will escape in the king's palace any more than all the other Jews. For if you remain completely silent at this time, relief and deliverance will arise for the Jews from another place. But you and your father's house will perish. Yet who knows whether you have come to the kingdom for such a time as this?"[33]

The booklet went on to describe many men who are famous for their walk of faith. God called each of them to obey Him in a special way. Each of them had to do it at great risk. Obedience turned out to be very costly to some of them. The end result, in each case, is that life is much better for each of us because of their faithfulness to the Lord's command.

I was horrified. God wanted me to obey Him and obey Him now. There was no question about what I had to do. I had to conform my

---

[33] *Esther 4:13-14*

life completely and literally to God's word and I had to do it while I was still in the Navy.

When the underway exercise was over, I acted out God's command to take Him literally at His word. I had some things to do to make it happen. So, I took care of those administrative things and published my religious stance to everyone and to every organization that it effected. The boundaries that obedience to God's word placed in my life began to mildly conflict with other's daily norms.

I continued to act faithfully upon the boundaries God placed in my life as I have to this day. I waited a few weeks however to formally ask for a religious accommodation. We were going through a change of command so I waited to submit my request until after the new commanding officer took the helm. The Chief Staff officer (sort of the executive officer under the Commodore) got wind of my not conforming to the norm. He called me into his office to rebuke me. I humbly and respectfully explained my convictions to him. I showed him that my convictions could be accommodated but it would take a little administrative record keeping adjustments. I explained that I had a formal religious accommodation request prepared and I would submit it after the change of command. He was perturbed but realized

Episode Eight

I had not done anything wrong. So, on November 6, 1996, I formally requested a religious accommodation. That is when my worst fears began to materialize. I went from being the honored subject matter expert in my field to being the target of ridicule and scorn. The details of the daily struggle, from that point onward, would distress the reader of this book too much. Suffice to say, the Navy put me in a situation where I had to choose to either abandon my convictions, or relinquish my career. I was challenged to deny Christ for the sake of sustenance. It was a choice between serving God or mammon.

Episode Nine

Freelance Human Being
March 1997

So! I obeyed God! And what did it get me? Unemployment!

"Count it all joy my brethren, when you fall into various trials knowing that the testing of your faith produces patience." James 1:2-3

From this point forward, you are going to read a story that has similarities with the children of Israel's trek to the Promised Land. I had a history of seeing God give tangible signs of His working in my situations. Up to this point however, I had no experience with having to truly rely on God for my survival. The provision of firewood was certainly a demonstration of God's power and His willingness to meet our basic needs. So, I had no excuse to not trust the Lord.

Please do not mock me as you continue to read. My wife and I often mocked the Israelite's constant complaining. We would say, " You would think these people would learn to trust God! I mean, how many times does He have to perform miracles before they believe Him." Well! I am beyond sorry that I ever gave in to that temptation to scorn them. I now know how easy it is to yield to our flesh when we are not walking in the Spirit. Like the children of Israel, I began to fear as soon as I perceived a potential catastrophe. I made whiny confessions about the doom that I thought loomed ahead. God, in His infinite mercy, would nevertheless sustain me again, and I would see my obvious shame.

As the day of my unemployment neared, I prayed to the Lord to give me tasking. It was bad enough that I was bringing shame upon my family by putting them in financial jeopardy. At least God could give me something noble to do so that my reputation would not be completely ruined. But to my dismay, God gave me a specific word that I was supposed to adhere to for my tasking. "Seek ye first the kingdom of God." ("And His righteousness" was no doubt implied).

I complained to the Lord about His word to me even though I realized that arguing with the Creator of the universe is very risky. I pleaded with the Lord for something more tangible. I wanted something that would make a show to others that I had significance, that I was not arbitrarily forsaking my obligations to support my family, and that would fulfill other's expectations of a credible Christian man of "faith." However, His Spirit bore witness with my spirit that "Seek ye first the kingdom of God", was all I was going to hear from Him.

AAAAARGH! I was not only frustrated, I was extremely fearful. How was I going to survive? How was I going to pay my mortgage? How was I going to eat? Now some of you would say, "What's the problem? Why don't you just go get a job?" Without going into detail in this book, just going and getting a job was no simple matter. The whole reason I was out of the Navy was the same reason I did not have access to conventional employment. God had placed an administrative barrier between me and employers. But on the positive side, I am extremely grateful that God had given me that barrier. Otherwise, I would not have been obedient to His word to seek first

Episode Nine

His kingdom. To save myself, I would have found a respectable employment position just like Jonah found a ship headed in the wrong direction. I really had very little option except to seek God daily to discover my tasking. That is when the miracles began to flow.

The first day out of the Navy, Wednesday, March 18, 1997, I woke up in the morning with the rising of the sun rather than to the nerve shattering buzzing of an alarm clock. Leslie and I lay in bed, staring at the ceiling. We discussed our mutual thoughts. The first feeling was, we were disappointed that it had not been just a bad dream. It was reality. I had no reason to get dressed. No reason to shave. There was nowhere I had to go, and no specific time to be there. Leslie asked me what I was going to do. I told her I was going to pray and seek first the kingdom of God. Our prayer time was one where we vented some of our exasperation. At the end of our prayers, we came to a point of resolution. Leslie needed to get up and do her daily activities. Nothing had changed for her. In my prayer time, God did not give me an exciting revelation about a new career. He just gave me peace. I was aware that there was a military surplus auction scheduled for the next day. I figured I could possibly buy some things to sell. The Lord gave me peace that it was a reasonable endeavor that He had no objection to. So I got up, got ready for the day, filled my coffee cup, kissed my wife and headed out the door to look at military surplus on the first day of my new adventure.

I arrived at the Defense Reutilization and Marketing Office (DRMO) in Norfolk, Virginia at about ten o'clock. It was a rather sunny and warm day for the season. Each of the warehouses still had the residual uncomfortable chill of the season's previous colder days. There were mostly industrial equipment and parts that I could not use. Some computer monitors looked in good condition. There were also some quality armoires that I thought would do well at a yard sale. I had written down the things that I thought were suitable for me to purchase. Then I continued to browse through the warehouse, merely for my own entertainment, since I had nothing better to do that day.

I got in a conversation with three men. I started to act business-like and I asked the men for their business cards. I thought I might be able to sell monitors to them, one at a time, that I bought in quantity. As we finished our conversation, another man who had been listening walked up and asked me if I would be at the auction the next day. He asked me if I knew how the auction worked. I began to explain it to him. He interrupted me because he really did not want to know the procedure. He wanted to see if I knew the procedure. He told me there were some filters that he needed but he was not able to attend the auction. He asked if I would be willing to bid for him and arrange shipment for the materials. I said, "This is for remuneration, right?" He confirmed that he intended to pay me for my services. I told him I agreed but I would have to draft a contract for the terms. He agreed and then realized that he did not know whether I was acting privately or on behalf of a company. So with an apologetic and a little confused look on his face he said, "What do you do? I mean, what is your business?"

On the first day of my new adventure I was asked the question of all questions. As soon as the gentleman started talking business, I immediately put on an air of professionalism. His question removed the mask I had donned. My countenance dropped and displayed perplexity. I could see that he noticed the change of my demeanor. I did not know what to say. I could try to describe the sort of business I was about to engage in but I knew it would falsely imply that it was some licensed company. How should I explain the truth? I considered telling him about my status as a man on his first day out of the Navy, but what kind of status is that? I was in a dilemma. The delay in my answering him was becoming very awkward. I knew I had to give him an answer immediately and it ought to be succinct. Then it dawned on me like a revelation. I first smiled and began to subtly laugh. I realized there was no better statement or title to describe my status. It caused me to sort of chuckle as I said, "I am a Freelance Human Being."

I summed my situation up with that declaration. I had an identity, a title, a status. It did not depend on any other person or organization lending their stamp or seal of approval or accreditation. I was whom God had made me, in the role He had given me, and free to do whatever the Lord willed, whenever He willed it. Relief and a sense of liberty swept over me. I felt as if I had just been promoted to the top of all ranks. God had just liberated me from my petty impulse to seek external credibility. I was now available to walk in my new role.

The man was taken back by my weird reply. I told him to never mind about my jesting but that I would be happy to serve him. I got his address, telephone, and fax number, and I went home to draft a contract and make all the arrangements. My new handle for email became from that point on, <u>freelancehumanbeing@…</u>

Episode Nine

When I got out of the Navy, we did not have any immediate pending doom since I had $3400.00 cash from my close-out Navy paycheck that had included payment for 30 days of accrued leave. I made a few dollars on buying and selling surplus. I made some money for bidding on, purchasing and shipping material on behalf of someone else. I had a few opportunities fixing computers, moving furniture and making household repairs. Yet, I was not making enough to recoup the money we were spending to keep our household of five sustained

A month after I was out of the Navy, I only had $1,600.00 left. By mid May, I found myself down to having the cash for one mortgage payment and a five-dollar bill. There were two weeks remaining before the mortgage payment was due. I had no prospects for commerce to pay for my other needs, except for eleven bunk-beds that I had purchased at my second auction. We were traveling around in cars that were becoming prone to breakdowns. So, I took two $20.00 bills and a $10.00 bill out of the mortgage envelope and put it in my wallet in case of an emergency. Other than that, all we had for "spending money" was the $5.00 bill.

It was time for our kids' end-of-season soccer party and my wife had gone ahead to the party at a friend's house. I followed a few minutes later in our car. On the way, I spotted a gentleman whom we know well as a very poor man, who is slightly disabled, with a hunched back and bad vision. I would often see him walking to work and I would pick him up and give him a ride. At the end of every ride, he would ask me for money. It was his standard behavior with everyone he knew. We had recently discovered that this man, (J) actually owned a very nice house that was left to him by his parents.

As soon as I saw (J) walking to work, I became resentful. There he was. Walking to his job. With his house paid for. With no family to support. I knew that if I picked him up to take him to work, he would expect me to give him money when I got him there. I told myself that he was better off than I was and he did not need me to give him a ride. Immediately, I recognized how rotten my attitude was. I knew in truth that giving him a ride was the right thing to do. I argued with my conscience. I realized that if I softened my heart and gave him a ride, I would feel further obligated to give him money when he asked. That is when I heard from the Lord. The Holy Spirit conveyed to me that I must continue to take care of (J) as one of the "least of these". [34] I responded to the Lord's will by gritting my teeth

---

[34] *Matthew 25:31-46*

and pulling over to offer (J) a ride.

Of course, he accepted my offer. (J) made himself comfortable and buckled up. I drove off and carried on the casual small-talk that was normal between us. Internally, I was really struggling with envy, covetousness, resentment, and anger. The Holy Spirit continued to bear down heavy on my heart. I was extremely frustrated because, "no way" did I want to give (J) any money. But God's voice was so strong. I knew it would be a major sin, with big ramifications if I was not obedient. I told the Lord silently in my prayer, sent up with a bad attitude attached: "Okay Lord! I will give him my last five dollars." With that settled, I drove on with resolve that I would do what God was asking of me. Even so, I was really having a difficult time trying to get my attitude in order.

We arrived at (J)'s workplace and I said, "Well, here we are!" (J) said, "I am a little early. I wanted to go into this store and get some coffee before I go into work. Do you have any change that I could have?" Well, I did not need to be a prophet to figure he would pop that question. However, I knew my obligation to him as one of "the least of these." I said, still grudgingly, "How is five dollars? Will that do?" (J) was pleasantly surprised and said, "Yes! That will be fine."

I reached into my pocket and pulled out my wallet. Then I made a horrible discovery. I had been keeping my $5 spending money under my wallet on a shelf in the kitchen. I presumed I had grabbed the loose $5 bill along with the wallet as I prepared to leave the house that morning. When I reached into my pocket, all I found was my wallet. I had left the $5 bill on the shelf. I opened my wallet to verify my thought and sure enough, only Hamilton and two Jacksons returned my gaze.

I realized that my bad attitude had set me up to be spiritually mocked. I saw right away that the minimum I had to give (J) was a $10 bill and I knew I had to give it to him. God had called me on my bad faith. Now smarty-pants David was going to be officially five dollars short of a house payment. For the first time in my life, I was going to have to literally trust God for my survival.

You would think I would take the opportunity, that God had presented, to humble myself. My flesh is pretty strong though. My next action was shameful. I knew (J) probably had money on him. I said, "All I have is a ten, do you have change?" Even though (J) responded the way I expected him to, my action was wicked and so was my heart. (J) reached to pull out his wallet to make change and then he realized his error. He tried to casually move his hand back so as to try to cover up the signal he sent to me that he actually had money. Now I had led (J) into a worse situation but this time his sin was on my shoulders. I relented and said "never mind. Just take the ten." (J) sheepishly thanked me and quickly left my car.

I was ashamed of myself. What good is it to do a "good deed" that is actually just bringing to light your sinful heart? I drove away confessing my sin and I pleaded for God's mercy. I acknowledged to the Lord that now I had to trust Him. I now had no way to rely upon myself. I understood though, that God would deliver me because of His faithfulness rather than my worthiness. I felt somewhat relieved that the Lord had used the situation to adjust my attitude.

I arrived at the soccer party much more than fashionably late. Right as I walked in the door, the hostess, Rhoda, asked me if we could use any potatoes. She somehow had an overabundance. We could use some potatoes and so Rhoda brought me a bag of them. God was already beginning to meet our physical need.

When I got home, I looked into the mailbox and found a check. My knee-jerk reaction was to try to imagine it as some sort of miracle but I knew that it was not. It was a check for $67.88 that I received monthly from my deceased Grandmother's trust. I started to calculate what needs the $67 would meet and also how I was going to cash the check. Then I caught myself and determined that I needed to give a tithe. I had never had to tithe on such a petty amount. I thought, "How do you tithe $67.88? I guess I'll give $6.78; or should I round it up to $ 6.79? Man this is petty. I should just give $7.00. That is a pretty small amount. Maybe I should give $10.00." I realized as I considered each of these things, that I had an internal spirit of hoarding. Considering to give a tithe should boost your spirit. But I was being grieved in my spirit as I struggled over which petty amount to give. Then it hit me. If I did not somehow get ten times $67.88, I was not going to survive. I needed to use the whole thing as a tithe. Then I got another revelation. I got a picture of what a first-fruit offering might be. I would be using the amount, $67.88, as a medium to express my faith. It was my tangible expression that I trusted God for my survival.

Since I was well aware that my natural tendency is to be fickle, I immediately endorsed the back of the check, "Pay to Restoration Church, for no remuneration." Once I wrote that endorsement, it would be very difficult for me to go back on my commitment of faith.

Trusting the Lord for the rest of that day was somewhat easier.

When I woke up on Sunday morning I understood that it was going to be a day of faith. I had a feeling that I had not learned enough yet. God might use the church service to teach me something else. During the service, when the offering plate came around, I still had a twinge of reluctance. When I placed the check into the plate I thought: "Well! Here it goes. I can't take it back now." Sadly, I was still struggling over believing God for my provision.

Immediately following the service, I was approached by a lady who asked, " David! I hear you are selling bunk-beds and I wanted to know if I could buy one." Her statement thrilled me. I had not even advertised the selling of the bunk-beds yet. Someone close to me, who knew I had the bunk-beds, told this lady of my intentions. The lady asked how much I was selling the bunk-beds for. At the time, I did not know the demand for bunk-beds. I wanted to sell them quickly in order to have money to feed my family. I told her forty-five dollars. In my mind I was thinking that God was already beginning to bless me. He'd sent me a customer without me having to advertise. I was beginning to get a sense of relief.

But then a big hole was shot in my presumption. The lady began to explain that her two children had been sleeping on the floor and having bunk-beds was the only way to fit two beds into their room. She then asked, "Can I pay you over time?" My face fell just a little bit. Her arrival was not a means for my survival. I had eleven bunk-beds and this lady needed one desperately. How could I hold my sister in Christ in the bondage of debt so that her children would not have to sleep on the floor? I had certainly enough faith that God would take care of me if He was able to use me to take care of this lady. I concluded that it was time to give another first-fruit offering. I responded to her in surrender. I said, "I'll give you a bunk-bed. You don't have to pay me." I realized there was a sound of reluctance in my voice so I stated with a more chipper demeanor, "I'd love to give you a bunk-bed. I've got plenty of them." Because I knew of my fickleness, I immediately made arrangements for delivery and installation.

The first-fruit bunk-bed offering had not been delivered but it had been committed. In my mind, I was stewing on the practical faith lesson that God was teaching me. During the previous twenty-four hours, I'd been aware of God's voice telling me to let go of those things that I was hanging on to for the means of my survival. God showed me that I had a severe lack of faith. Though I had given away $10.00 to (J), $67.88 to the offering plate and $45.00 dollars worth of bunk-beds to a needy woman, for a total of $122.88, the Lord had returned to me about $2.88 in potatoes. I became very thankful for those potatoes as the Lord's sign to me that He would meet our need. As my wife and I met each other at the car with the children, we began to talk about what God had been teaching us that day. Leslie told me that the Lord showed her that she needed to have more faith and really believe Him for our needs. As we got into the car and drove home, I began to tell Les about what God had shown me. I told her about the different ways God challenged me to give to Him. We both began to weep as we responded to God's healing and maturing work in our hearts. The kids sat quietly in the back seat listening to our conversation.

We pulled up into the driveway and paused to finish our conversation. As we turned our heads away from each other preparing to exit the car, we noticed something taped to the front door of our house. We mentioned to each other that it might be something to worry about. We approached the door with apprehension. Possibly our dogs had been making noise while we were at church and had disturbed the neighbors. We removed an envelope from the front door. It was labeled "The Carmichaels". I opened the envelope and found a letter and $120.00 cash. I was shocked and somewhat relieved. Then it occurred to me. God had returned to me every penny that I had given him in the last 24 hours. He returned it to me in cash and potatoes. He'd done it incrementally so that I would be getting lessons from His teachings along the way.

The letter said, "I have no need of a bull from your stall or of goats from your pens, for every animal of the forest is mine, and the cattle on a thousand hills. I now every bird in the mountains, and the creatures of the field are mine. If I were hungry I would not tell you, for the world is mine, and all that is in it... ... Sacrifice thank offerings to God, fulfill your vows to the most High, and call upon me in the day of trouble; I will deliver you, and you will honor me."

He went on to say, "Dad told me to take one of the cows to market and give you the proceeds, so here it is." Right away, in the minds of both my wife and I, we understood that God had spoken to someone else on our behalf. God was very aware of our need and He was actively doing work that we could not see in order to meet our need. We were also both convicted that God was blessing us even though we had been unbelieving. Someone, with more faith than us, was willing to listen to God's voice and sell something that may have been valuable to them, specifically in order to give us the money. We both sat down on the stoop and wept profusely. We were encouraged, yet envious, that someone else had 'ears to hear' and was willing to obey.

Episode Ten

No Hoarding Allowed

Getting $120.00 plus potatoes may seem to some as more of a coincidence rather than a miracle. Some may even give it the credit of being providence (preordained by God spinning up His plan and letting it go). I assure you that it was more than that. Consider the words of the anonymous giver. "He (...his Father who owns the cattle on a thousand hills) **told** me to sell one and give you the proceeds. I can safely presume that the word cattle in this application was figurative since we do not know anyone who actually has access to cattle. No doubt, the writer considers his "possessions" to be really owned by God. I get the impression, by the words used, that God "the Holy Spirit" spoke directly to the spirit of the person who gave us the gift. The person had to take an action outside of his daily-norm, to sell his goods solely for our benefit. The written message to us, tied to the timeliness of the gift, sent a much bigger message. God met our need in keeping with His word, and glorified Himself while doing it. As we progress in our story, you will see other "coincidences" which are <u>not</u> coincidences. They are not merely providence, but instead are <u>absolutely</u> Divine intervention.

After having a lesson on letting go of those physical things that I naturally rely upon for my own salvation, my financial situation was no better. It was technically worse. However, I was not just proactively trusting the Lord for my physical salvation, I was becoming more natural at it. I was less panicky and more confident in my routine of getting up in the morning, seeking first the kingdom of God, and then doing what I was led to do by the Holy Spirit. Sometimes He would give me work for pay, sometimes work for free, and sometimes I was able to just do ministry.

On a weekday, I was visiting with the staff at my church. While I was there, a lady (D.) asked me about what I was doing those days. By this time, the grapevine around the church had communicated, to those with an itching ear, that David Carmichael, half-cocked, had gotten out of the Navy for the sake of some warped religious objection. Nevertheless, I assumed in my conversations with folks that they did not have a predetermined negative opinion of my motives. I told (D.) that I was getting up every morning, praying, and doing what God showed me to do. I told her about the surplus sales I had done and some of the odd jobs I had. She asked me if I was looking for a job and then told me that a seafood company was hiring people to drive their delivery trucks. I asked her how much it paid. She said six dollars an hour. I then said that I would pass on that one. If I got a job for six dollars an hour, I would die. I was being semi-literal. I had a family of five to feed and a house payment. Every hour I spent in a truck would be an hour that I did not have available to make the money I needed. (D.) rebuked me saying, "Well you can't just sit around praying, you need to do something. **A job is not just going to come up and knock on your door.**"

I felt like a bum. The rebuke made me question my motives and my mode of operation. So I staggered a bit from the blow and evaluated my status. I certainly would have taken the job if the Holy Spirit affirmed to me that it was the right thing to do despite the math. At that point though, taking the driver job for meager pay would be an act of desperation. I sensed, after diligent prayer, that God had something else for me and I needed to be available for it.

Not too many days later, I had finished my time of prayer and taking care of the things by the leading of the Holy Spirit. I was taking a break from my tasks of the day and was visiting with my wife in the kitchen. Unexpectedly, there was a **knock on the door**.

Olivia Fulcher came by to visit. I can't remember why. I think she came by just for the sole purpose of visiting. I sat down at a table in the kitchen with her, while my wife stood at the stove continuing to cook a meal. Olivia was in our church home group and had been a great encouragement to us. She too was in poverty and had been recently blessed by the Lord and His divine intervention with a job that paid well and was very satisfying to her. She just came by to give us an update on God's blessings. She asked me the very popular question of the time, "What are you doing David?" I gave her the same answer that I gave (D.). I included saying some things about my recent escapades of buying surplus computers and monitors and fixing them up to sell. She then asked me to tell her what I had done while in the Navy. I told her about my training as a sonarman, my time as an instructor, and all the other experience I had in the nearly seventeen years. She was astounded at the things I included about my experience. She told me that she needed to talk to her boss about me. I would be perfect for his company. They developed training tailored to the needs of the requesting companies and organizations. They hired instructors on a full-time or part-time basis who had the subject matter expertise for the particular training scenario. She asked me if I had a résumé. I had one in my briefcase that was sitting on the table in front of me.

The next day, Olivia asked me to come in to talk to her boss. Her boss is either a guy who wears a face like he hates everybody or he just despised me alone. He made it very clear that he was not interested in allowing me to get in on his program. Nevertheless, Olivia was very encouraging and she said that her boss just needed a chance to get to know me. She told me that they had a contract teaching computer building and other related information to "new-hires" at a local computer manufacturer. Olivia arranged for me to come and watch how they presented the course. That way, I could prepare myself to show her boss that I could do the job. She escorted me to Gateway and introduced me to the other instructors. She made it seem to them as if I was already on staff. I sat in on the first hour-and-a-half of training and I visited with the other instructors during one of their breaks. I fit in with them really well. One of the instructors, Bill Quast, asked me about my background. We had very similar backgrounds and related well together. I told Bill how his boss reacted to me. I asked Bill if I could get a chance to demonstrate my abilities. I asked him to let me do the review at the end of the session that night. He thought about it a while and then agreed.

The classroom is the environment where I find myself operating in the gifts God has given me. All the instructors were shocked. I did the review as smoothly as if I had been doing it for months. Bill said he could not have done better himself. They all went back and told Ron, the boss, that I was a natural and he needed to add me to his instructor pool.

Ron's business subcontracted to the State community college. The Commonwealth of Virginia was actually the one who paid me for my instructor contracts. Thus, I had to go through the Continuing Adult Education office to get my checks. When I went to get my first check, a representative from the community college interviewed me. I told her about my Navy career and my activities ministering to adults and youth at my church and in my home. Jo listened to everything I said in order to see what types of contracts she could secure now that I was in her instructor pool. She asked me if my ministry experience had equipped me to teach a stress management course. I told her that the training I received in the Navy as well as my ministry experience made me well equipped. That was all she needed to hear. She gave me the curriculum and told me when and where to report. I was to teach the class to civilians who were stressed because they were being laid-off from the Navy because their jobs were being eliminated.

I examined the stress management curriculum and found it to come up empty. The learning objectives seemed well suited to the titled course but the outline did not support the objectives. It had some overly simplistic definitions and a limited list of symptoms. It gave breathing and mind exercises from yoga as a solution for stress relief.

The course, as written, could only provide the students a waste of time away from their vanishing office tasks. It addressed over-commitment of their time and resources. These students had a more tangible affliction. They were about to be cut-off from their source of livelihood. In their minds eye, 'No livelihood? No life!' Their internal stressor was <u>fear</u>.

The Bible has a more suitable answer:

"You will keep him in perfect peace, whose mind is stayed on You, because he trusts in you."[35]

---

[35] *Isaiah 26:3*

"Be (stressed) for nothing. But in everything by prayer and supplication, with thanksgiving, let your requests be made known to God; and the peace of God which surpasses all understanding, will guard your hearts and minds through Christ Jesus."[36]

"For God has not given us a spirit of fear, but of power and of love, and of a sound mind."[37]

"...do not worry about your life, what you will eat; nor about the body, what you will put on.... and which of you by worrying can add one cubit to his stature? If then you are not able to do the least, why are you anxious for the rest?... O you of little faith? And do not seek what you should eat or what you should drink, nor have an anxious mind...."[38]

The state was paying me for a stress relief course. I was given the details of the stress that my students needed to be relieved from. God has already given us the answers for stress relief. Since I have a conscience, I could not feed the students what I was handed by the State. I gave them the truth.

I took the course objectives and considered them as they related

---

[36] *Philippians 4:6-7*
[37] *II Timothy 1:7*
[38] *Luke 12:22,25,26,28,29*

to the word of God. I considered the most likely practical experiences of the students and used them as "hypothetical" examples. Then I converted the course into one based upon the nature of man and our choice between fear and faith. I had to do a lot of praying before I went into the course.

It was a smash. Unbeknown to me, one of the attendees was a representative from the government who was acting in a social worker role. She had taught many stress management courses over the years. At the end of the course, she told me her qualifications and then asked me about mine. At first, I thought she was challenging my qualifications to teach the course. It turned out however, she thought I was a professional psychologist. It was the most profound and refreshing stress management course she had ever experienced and she wanted to know how I had acquired my expertise. I told her about my military training in victim crisis intervention, my ministry experience, and how I approached the course based upon the specific needs of the audience. She was very satisfied by my response and showed great interest. Then I told her that the real difference between my course and the government's, was that mine was based upon the principles found in God's word. I explained that the secular curriculum offered no solutions, only topical distractions. She was almost stunned by what I said, though you could tell by her facial expressions that she had become enlightened. Through the class, she had been exposed to God's kingdom. The Spirit of the Lord had been upon the teaching. She sensed it but had not understood what it was.

God had been faithful to give me a job that fit the mold in which He had made me. The pay started at $25.00 an hour and it was somewhat negotiable depending on the job. God had made the job come to me. It literally <u>knocked on my door</u>.

Shortly after getting the computer building and Navy contracts, I had opportunities to expand my part-time business. One of the problems I encountered was the fact that I did not have email. When you hand somebody your business card selling your ability to teach about or fix computers, they find it very strange if you do not have an email address. They question your credibility. The reason I did not have email was because I did not have a computer that would support it. I did not have a modem with a sufficient data transfer rate. My computer had a 386 processor with 16 Mega-Hertz (MHz) speed. At the time, a 386 processor with 33 MHz speed was the minimum I needed to run my free email software. Not only that, it had a 40 Megabyte hard-drive that did not have sufficient space to actually load the free email software. The computer had only enough memory to store the operating system, a multipurpose word processing spreadsheet database program, and my small files. I was not the only one that had a need. Leslie had been home-schooling our children and desperately needed a computer. Just like the incident of the firewood, I began to get a sense that God was going to meet my need with miraculous provision. I can't remember if I actually heard God speak to me, but for certain I knew that I was supposed to depend on God to meet that specific need.

One day, as usual, I got up and prayed. I asked God what I was supposed to do that day. I had some things to make myself productive, but nothing on my list was absolutely necessary. There might be something that Lord could impress upon me to do for His kingdom. I did not get any specific direction that morning. However, I received a telephone call from someone who asked me if I could install a compact-disc drive in her computer. She told me that she had money and would pay me for my services. I had a general rule of not giving a "yes" answer unless I first told them the exact amount they would have to pay. I would not say yes until they agreed to my terms. So as she began to speak, I began to listen and I began to pray. I sought from the Lord what I should charge my customer. As I prayed, the Lord showed me that I was not supposed to take money for the job.

As you read this book you may get the sense that being an obedient guy would eventually be easy at some point. But again, I struggled. I argued. I explained to God how important was for me to do work that actually earned money so that I could take care of my family. In the back of my mind, I knew my wife was becoming very sensitive to me doing work for free while we had many needs of our own. While the lady was speaking on the phone, God showed me that He wanted me to trust him for provision and just do what He told me. So, I agreed with the Lord to install a compact disk drive for free.

When I went to the lady's house, I found her typing out a document on her computer with her kids doing their school-work in the kitchen. She got up to allow me to do my computer surgery. When I finished, I got up to leave and told her that her computer was ready to go. As I began to leave, she reached for her pocketbook and pulled out a certain sum of money and asked me if it was enough. I told her that I would not take her money. I explained that God had told me that I was not to take any money from her. She, on one hand, was obviously grateful but acted in the standard courtesy of trying to dissuade me from refusing her offer. I told her that, under the circumstances, I could not take any money without being in sin. She capitulated and then turned to her kitchen chair and picked up a motherboard. She said, "At least let me give you this. You've got to take something." She handed me a motherboard that had the processor and short-term memory I needed to run my email software. Immediately I felt a sense of satisfaction and relief. When I examined the motherboard, I realized that it would not exactly fit into my computer case. I resolved that I would borrow a tool to cut things out of my computer case to make room for the larger motherboard. Internally I sensed that it really was not an answer from God. It did not totally meet my need. But logically, it was a step in the right direction. Of course, I knew my wife would be satisfied to know that I was doing something to solve our computer deficiencies.

As I was driving the mile back to my house, I spent time in praise and worship, thanking God for his gift. I was overjoyed and professed to myself that "The workman was worthy of his wages." With that thought, immediately to my horror, I began hear the voice of the Lord. He told me I was not allowed to keep the motherboard. I was supposed give it away to a young man who I told I would help to build a computer. I began to argue with the Lord. "But Lord! Can't You see that I have a need?. Can't You see that it is necessary for me have email. Les needs it for homeschool. I've got to start taking care of my family first. Otherwise, I'll be nothing more than an infidel." Before those thoughts could leave my mind, I knew immediately that God was not happy with my hoarding heart. God spoke to me, "Don't you think I know your need? Don't you think I'm able to meet your need? Don't you realize that I want to bless you beyond that which you can imagine? You need to stop hoarding. Trust me."

As the Lord concluded his admonition to me, I pleaded with Him. "Lord OK. I have been hoarding. Please forgive me. But Lord! Talk to my wife. She's not going to be happy about this."

By the time I resolved my wresting with the Lord, I had pulled into my driveway. I went through the front door and Leslie greeted me with a big smile on her face. She looked at the motherboard in my hand. She got a bigger smile on her face and asked me what kind of processor it had. I told her and she was gleaming. She then asked me if it had the memory we needed. By my hesitation and my lackluster response, she knew that something was wrong. Leslie looked at me and figured it out. Her demeanor changed from satisfaction to consternation. She said very sternly, "You're going to give it away. Aren't you?" What could I say? I didn't say anything and it would not have mattered anyway. Leslie started boisterously venting the same things that I had pleaded to the Lord during my prayer argument in the car. She asked me if I realized I needed to work for money. She told me that I needed to start taking care of my family. I was taking care of everybody else but them. The things she said were true. I was exasperated because I was not able to apologize. I was not able to change my mind. I began to plead with her using the words that the Lord had used to rebuke me. I said, "Les! Don't you think God knows our need? Don't you realize that He wants to bless us beyond that which we can imagine? We just need to trust Him?" I explained to her that the same things she just said had come to my mind when the Holy Spirit told me that I was supposed to give the motherboard away. Leslie was understandably frustrated.

Then things got scary. "Well if you say God is going to bless us, you tell God.…" Her words frightened me. I had a sinking suspicion that we might all be hit by lightning in a very few seconds. I thought she was angry with God and was blaspheming Him. So, I distracted my thoughts so I could not focus on what she was saying. I did not realize that she was essentially praying. She was crying her need out to God. Leslie told God that she needed a computer with a large enough hard-drive to store educational software and all the other things we needed. It needed to have enough short-term memory to run the newer programs. It needed to have a modem so we could get email. It needed to have a compact-disc drive and speakers. Lastly, the case needed to be a tower so that it could stand alongside her table in the dining room, rather than on it. Oh! It also needed to be good looking. She began to cry out and say that she did not want an ugly computer in her dining room (the only place that it would be useful for homeschool purposes).

While I was ignoring what seemed to me like ranting and raving, the telephone rang. I wondered what I should do. If I answered it, whoever was calling would overhear my wife. However, the combination of the loud ringing and the loud raging was growing unbearable. I rushed to pick up the receiver and I baffled the background sound with my hand around the mouthpiece as I curtly greeted the caller. I hoped the call would be for Leslie so that she would have to compose herself. The call was for me.

It was Olivia. She asked if she could come over and talk to me. I asked her when, and she told me about 15 minutes. I considered my wife's state of mind and I thought it would be good to have somebody come to the house. It might provide a little distraction. I believed about 15 minutes would be long enough to allow Les to cool down a little bit. I answered to Olivia that fifteen to twenty five minutes from then would be good. I told Les that Olivia was coming over to visit. Les asked what she wanted to visit for and I explained that I didn't know. "She just said she wanted to talk." Leslie told me that I could talk to Olivia in the living room. She did not want to talk to anybody.

I wished I could relieve my wife of her frustration, but I was helpless. In about twenty minutes, Olivia showed up. When I invited Olivia in, my wife was not her usual hospitable self. I escorted Olivia to the living room couch and hoped she did not notice my wife's demeanor. After about fifteen minutes of talking about various things, finally, Olivia said, "Let me tell you why I came over to talk to you. I was praying and asking God who I should give my computer to. Immediately the Lord told me 'David'."

I said, "Ooh! Ooh! Leslie! Come in here a minute. I had to repeat it a few times to motivate my wife to come into the room. I told Olivia to say her statement again with my wife listening. After Olivia restated her story, I expected Leslie to become excited that God was performing a miracle before our very eyes and ears. To my disappointment, Leslie's demeanor seemed to become even more stern. Les later told me why she was motivated to react that way.

She understood how much poorer Olivia was compared to us. What kind of computer could Olivia be giving to us? Leslie was thinking that the computer was probably destined for the trash can. She thought that Olivia was being naive, thinking she was doing a good deed giving her junk to us. With Les's worse than dismal show of appreciation, I did my best to encourage Olivia in her gift. Leslie returned to her work in the kitchen and I asked Olivia when I should go to her house to get the computer. She told me right away.

I went with my two oldest kids, Bethany and Jesse, into Olivia's apartment. I asked Olivia where the computer was. She pointed to some black trash bags that were in her kitchen. She said, "I put the computer in bags so the bugs will not get into your house. I know how tidy a housekeeper Leslie is and I don't want to give her my bugs." I did not understand how trash bags would keep bugs out of our house. If there were bugs in the house, there were probably bugs in the computer.

I got my crew to help me load the computer into our van. I thanked Olivia profusely and drove home. I was very excited by what she gave to us. When we got home, we carried the bags into the kitchen placed them on a table. At this point, I did not know that Les had believed the computer was a piece of junk headed for the garbage can. When she saw me bring the parts in trash bags, it confirmed her suspicion. She was angry. She said, "What are you doing putting that junk there? I don't want that in my kitchen. Take that out to the garage." I was shocked, confused and exasperated. Had she gone over the edge? Was the strain of our poverty and my seemingly ill-fated philanthropy too much to bear? I began to plead with her to not be so upset.

While I was speaking to her, I began to open one of the trash bags. When Leslie saw the Gateway computer tower that appeared, she covered her face with her hands and gasped. She said, "It's a gateway?" I said "yes!" She was suddenly solemn and silent. Then she asked, "Does it have a large hard drive?" I said "yes!" After another pause, "Does it have enough memory?" I said "yes!" With her eyes starting to tear, "Does it have a CD?" I said "yes!" I then told her that it had a modem as well. With her voice cracking a little she asked, "Does it have speakers?" I had to look, and then I said "Yes, it even has speakers!" Leslie began to cry as she started to get the full realization of how good God had been to us. It got even better. After we put the components in place, we found that not only was the case a tower, it was tall enough to reach evenly with her table. Not only did the computer not take up too much space on the desk, the height of the tower gave us more working area. We could place the telephone on it nice and even with the height of the desk. But wait! There's more! The case and monitor were very good looking (relatively speaking).

Since I refused to listen to Leslie's tirade, I did not realize she had described the computer I brought into the house in trash bags. While she was crying out to God, she was visualizing what she needed and what she expected to see if He really intended to bless us. While she was speaking, Olivia was dialing. God even provided a beautiful irony. The computer came in trash bags. Leslie presumed something our beloved impoverished Olivia could give us would be only worthy of a dumpster destiny.

In the winter months beginning the year 2003, Olivia came to visit us. We then heard the rest of the story. The Holy Spirit spoke to her two weeks prior to her calling us on the telephone. Because of her bug problem, she placed the computer in trash bags and sealed them after spraying the inside with insect killer. She waited long enough for the bugs and their larvae to be destroyed before she let us take the computer into our house. Right about the time I finished pleading with Leslie, Olivia had been working in her kitchen and noticed the trash bag encased computer. She felt a compulsion to immediately telephone us to arrange for its delivery. We learned that God had actually arranged to meet our need two weeks before our spiritual wrestling match.

We have discovered over the years that God did not just give us that computer to benefit us. We can see in retrospect that His intent was to bless many people to come. I have told this story many times in order to give people courage to believe upon the Lord. And since that time: I have received dozens upon dozens of computers; used many of them as a means to minister the gospel; and have given dozens upon dozens away. Through the Holy Spirit speaking directly to Olivia, and speaking directly to me, God used another opportunity to glorify Himself and further His kingdom.

Episode Eleven

Freelance Disciple

The title of this book "Faith - The Final Frontier" is very significant. In this book you have read, and will read, about times when I heard from God. In every case, it required me to have to decide whether I was going to follow God's trail or stop in my tracks because the potential consequences seemed too costly. That syndrome is much like frontier exploration. Explorers proceed on their journey at great risk. They have no idea what they are going to find on their travels. They can guarantee that there will be some huge obstacles. They do not know what will ultimately come from their journey. Will they have discovered new things that they can teach others about? Will they accomplish something that everyone else coming after them can benefit from? Will they deplete their resources or injure themselves so that they are physically unable to do anything useful from that point forward? Will they even survive the journey?

When God asks me to do something, my will is the cost of obedience. To carry out an act of faith, my desires have to die. How painful it will be to yield to God's bidding to let go depends on how tightly I am holding on to my Earthly lifeboat. From the day I was made to walk the plank (figuratively - On March 17, 1997), and had to choose between the blade and being cast adrift, my life boat seemed very unstable and lacked adequate provision. God used Olivia to throw me a life-line. I was able to trade my depleted life raft in for a real boat through the instructor contracts. Then Olivia's gift of a computer seemed to provide a sail. I found myself beginning to ride on fair winds and following seas. However, just as I began to make what seemed to me as God-speed, God told me to step out of the boat again.

After getting a good computer, I was able to pursue my newly found freelance instructor vocation in earnest. Actually, the vocation pursued me and I was now able to keep pace with the demand. By

Episode Eleven

August of that year, 1997, my freelance instructor vocation had become lucrative. I was beginning to have so many requests for contracts that I had to choose which ones to turn down. It was good to be able to start experiencing relief from poverty. Then I began to get that unnerving sense that God was calling me again to a greater commitment.

My experience with the stress management course, and the ministry of the gospel that resulted, had a deep impact on me. I was moved by how desperately people needed to know God through His Son Jesus Christ. I understood God's desire to set the captives free. My approach to relating to the students in all my courses changed dramatically. I worked very hard to make sure I was giving each student much more teaching quality and personal attention than they could ever expect. My opportunities to effectively present the gospel in one-on-one conversations rapidly increased. I found myself truly being a minister of the gospel, cleverly disguised as a freelance instructor.

The majority of my teaching opportunities involved computer training. Most of my students fell into one of three categories. They were retirees who had enough time and money on their hands; they were employees of a large company that was paying for the course; or they were someone who was having the course paid for by a grant from the government. Some of my students were in their forties and had been recently laid off from a job that they expected to hold until retirement. When they tried to get re-employed, all the jobs they would be considered for required computer skills. These people were being displaced and replaced by teenagers who had learned the skills in public school; and could work for much less money since they did not have a household to maintain.

God showed me that He wanted me to take my gifts as an instructor and use them in an evangelism ministry. God stirred my heart very powerfully with a vision to start free computer classes to meet people's physical needs. It was a means to strike up an opportunity to meet their spiritual needs as well. My struggle with the Lord over this was intense. It was bad enough that He had gotten me out of my decent paying Navy career. Now He wanted me to give up my current means of livelihood. As I tried to disregard the tugging at my heart, the sense that it was God's will became more assured. I began to writhe in anguish internally. I thought I had come to the place where I had given up my hold on Earthly things to trust in the

Lord. By my unwillingness to yield, I knew that my personal assessment was wrong. I struggled with the same fears that I had when God laid the burden on my heart which caused the end of my Navy career. I asked the Lord to have mercy on me because of the suffering it would bring upon my wife and children. I pleaded with God to remove the call, but I had no doubt that it was His mandate.

I slowly began to capitulate. I sought from the Lord direction on how to raise support before beginning the mission. I got more fearful news. I was not supposed to be spending my time raising support, I was supposed to do His tasking. It was a "just do it" mandate. I needed to trust Him to provide for our needs. That was the last thing I wanted to hear. I started my typical bargaining and rationalizing with the Lord to try to get a reprieve. How many irrational acts could I engage in before my family and my church disowned me? I pleaded with the Lord to let me do at least one thing that made sense. The Lord let me know that was not His plan. I had to believe Him and trust Him. It was His plan and not mine.

As I did with the edict I got from the Lord while in the Navy, I continued to put off making a decision. I had acknowledged to the Lord that I knew what He wanted me to do, but I did not tell my wife.

Also, I did not take any action that was consistent with what God was calling me to. I continued to negotiate teaching contracts that would run well into the first quarter of calendar year 1998. I knew I was pulling a Jonah act as soon as I started to respond to those longer-term requests. I was in the sin of rebellion and I knew it. I really did not trust God. I really feared everything else more than I feared Him. I was deeply grieved over my sin but I pressed on trying to distract myself while imploring God to relieve me of the burden of my new assignment.

Like Jonah, God loved me enough to head me off at the pass. While I was wrestling with the vision God had given me and simultaneously locking-in contracts that were taking me to Tarshish, God intervened. On a Thursday at the end of August, I realized I had taken on too many contracts to handle myself. It gave me so much distraction that God's call was not even rating as much as a back-seat status. On Friday however, all my contracts from September through the first quarter of the next year were suddenly cancelled. In a flash, I found myself without any work at all. God showed me that <u>He</u> was in control and that <u>my</u> success was solely dependent upon <u>His</u> discretion. Fortunately the catastrophe coincided with a weekend seminar at my church. I had Friday, Saturday and Sunday to pray and repent. I prayed a prayer much like Jonah. I admitted that God showed His mercy toward me by bringing the calamity that humbled me. I acknowledged to the Lord that He had spoken, I had heard, and I would obey.

That Sunday night I told my cell group, led by our Senior Pastor, about the ministry that God had called me to. I cannot tell you how my wife took it. She was nowhere near being over the trauma of me losing my Navy career. No one else was over it either. By this time however, no one was really shocked. They had begun to almost expect something like it. I had no idea how I would survive. I resolved to do what God had bid of me even though I thought it would lead to financial catastrophe. But God was really good. On Monday, I received several telephone calls and landed contracts that gave me all the work I needed through the month of December. When I was asked to consider some contracts that started in January, I declined. I told them I would be teaching classes for free in order to have an opportunity to share the Gospel of Jesus Christ. They tried to get me to work their contracts around my ministry. I knew that God wanted me to whole-heartedly commit myself to His calling and His provision. So, I stood firm on my refusal. I was committed.

The question came to my mind, "By what authority?" Who am I to announce and oversee an operational public ministry? The obvious Biblical no-brainer is that I was called and given authority in the great commission.[39] However, men are often concerned about education, accreditation, and licensing. How could I be accepted as a credible minister of the gospel without a formal degree or certification? I had challenged God about this issue in 1993 and He responded to me that He would be my accreditation. I know it is right that a man or woman be affirmed by their church leadership. There should be someone besides yourself that can, and will, affirm that you are firmly rooted in the Lord and called for the ministry. In my eyes, based upon Biblical precepts, it was sufficient and necessary for me to get affirmation from the Elders of my church.

I asked my senior Pastor, Leonard Riley, if he could arrange for me to meet with Elders. I wanted to explain the ministry that I knew God had called me to, and to ask for their affirmation. We met at Sammy and Nicks on Mercury Boulevard in Hampton, Virginia. The Elders were a bit wary of me because of the comparatively radical

---

[39] *Matthew 28:19-20*

steps I had recently taken that completely changed my life situation. Some of them had not gotten first-hand explanations from me about my motives. They had only heard from others. So I approached the meeting with a bit of trepidation. I reviewed the history of my salvation, my walk in Christ, my development in ministry during my tenure at the church, and my knowledge that God intended me to commit myself to ministry. I then told them about my recent work experience. I explained that God wanted me to use my talents as a means to produce opportunities to evangelize. I asked them if they would lay hands on me and "set me apart" for the ministry.

Brother Red Parker, a very practical man, told me he had no question about my commitment and zeal for the Lord but, "...you can't just go out and be a freelance minister." I remained stoic facially but internally I recognized some humor in his statement. Jesus taught us, basically, 'just do it' with regard to living in, and preaching, the kingdom of God. I also was happily stirred by his use of the term "freelance minister." Had I taken the comment out of context I might have been tempted to protest. However, we all knew what he meant by his beautifully succinct statement. There were some conventional and practical things that needed to be considered and addressed.

Who would I be accountable to? What kind of things needed to be done to establish a ministry that would stand the test of government scrutiny? The Elders of Restoration Church could not lend their good name in support of something unless they knew it truly was credible in its practice.

So, I explained the organization structure of our ministry that would name Bro. Leonard Riley (then Senior Pastor of Restoration Church) as the Elder of the ministry. He would be the one I was accountable to spiritually. Several men with good standing at the church would be named as ministry council members. They would be the ones that would give me counsel regarding the daily operations of the ministry. I would publish a declaration in the newspapers that announced the name and mission of the ministry. Then I would begin testing out the ministry concept at our own church for our own neighbors. I would make sure that I was submitted to my church leadership and that there was a way for me to be 'kept in check'. I told them that ultimately, I hoped they would provide financial support just like they do for other missionaries. The bottom line was, I wanted them to: bring me before the body of Christ at our church; affirm that I had been called to the ministry; and lay hands on me to set me apart for the ministry.

The Pastors and Elders admitted to one another that God had his hand on my life. They still needed to maintain a 'wait and see' posture regarding providing financial support or embracing the church name with my unorthodox ministry venture. They did agree to lay hands on me, before the congregation, to set me apart for the ministry of the gospel in November of 1997.

So, all was set for me to act out the vision God had given me. Now the big looming problem. We had no tangible hope for sustenance. My Fall teaching contracts gave us just enough to get by. How were we to survive from January onward?

Somehow, we survived 1997, but we were in abject poverty. When it came to thanksgiving time, we were extremely thankful that we had food. God used others to feed us well. We were given turkeys and plenty of other food. It was quite amazing to be able to have a feast to enjoy on Thanksgiving despite our lowly financial circumstances. Christmas was a different story however. There were some administrative complications at the community college and I had not received money for my most recent teaching contracts. Come mid-December, we had barely enough food to survive the month and we had nothing to give anybody else for Christmas, let alone our own children. Not only did we not have money for gifts, we did not have money to buy winter coats that were needed for our kids. We knew our need, we were ashamed of it, and we did not tell anyone about it.

We enjoyed making Christmas decorations to glorify Christ, and made them as festive as possible. Unlike the previous years however, there were no gifts for anybody. My wife was able to prepare a gift for Jesus by making something special for somebody who needed a blessing. God had many times before then brought money in the nick of time so we could purchase the things we needed. In this instance, we waited for the provision and it never came.

On Christmas Eve, the kids were put to bed knowing they would not have any presents to open in the morning except from one of their grandmothers. It seemed to me that the kids accepted it fairly well. It provided a good opportunity to focus on the true meaning of Christmas as a celebration of the Savior's birth. It was not so hard for me because I knew that there was nothing I could do to change the situation. I had worked hard to keep us surviving to that point. It was very difficult for my wife who has an innate desire to bless her children. She wants to give them the same opportunities that others have. We did our best to keep the faith. However, our situation did not bode well for a family who would soon have Dad, the "bread winner", now teaching for free.

After the kids were put to bed, Leslie and I visited together contemplating our situation. We mourned our situation somewhat, yet we also confessed that God had been good and that He no doubt would continue to be good. We comforted one another and began to prepare what we could for some Christmas morning festivities.

Then, there came a knock on the door. It was an emissary from a gift-giving cooperative that clandestinely accumulates gifts every Christmas to give a needy family. They had planned to give to some needy families who all of the sudden no longer had the need. In the last hour, somebody who knows us intimately suggested that some of the gifts be passed on to us. The gift givers decided, by the leading of the Lord, that all the gifts should come our way. There were so many gifts unloaded out of several cars, that they covered the front half of the living room and blocked our entry into the dining room. We had never then, nor since, seen so many presents in one place. One of the gifts was a beautiful, high quality, winter coat that fit Bethany perfectly and really nice coats that fit the boys too. We had presents that we could also give to other people.

When my kids woke up in the morning, they experienced a sharp contrast to their expectations. God had again demonstrated the definition of irony. What they considered would be the sparsest Christmas celebration of their young lives became abundant beyond human imagination. "Wow!" – was the word of the day. My second child and oldest son Jesse summed it up pretty well in a document he composed for school not long afterward:

The Best Christmas Ever

Christmas at our house is usually the best time of the year. On Christmas Eve our friends come over and we act out the Nativity. We dress up like Mary, Joseph, the shepherds, and the wisemen while Daddy reads the Christmas story. We act out the parts as Daddy reads them. A lot of times friends and family come on Christmas day. We thank God for sending his son into the world, and we read the Christmas story sitting around the crackling fire, drinking spicy warm wassail. Mom makes a great big breakfast and sometimes we eat cake to celebrate Jesus' birthday. Then we tear into all the wonderful gifts.

Last year my dad got out of the Navy so we had no extra

money. Nobody was even coming to visit us. We had to make Christmas presents because we could not afford to buy them. To give to others, so that we were not thinking of just ourselves, we sent a shoebox Christmas to a needy child. I wasn't expecting many gifts, but I was hoping for something special. I didn't even have trouble getting to sleep because I probably wouldn't get many presents. So I went to bed sad.

I woke up hopeful but not expecting much. I went downstairs surprised to see the huge, colorful mountain of presents! It was 10 feet wide and up to my waist! I wondered how many were for me?

When it was finally time to open presents, we each took a turn unwrapping a gift. There were huge ones, medium sized ones and teeny little ones. As we opened them we realized they were all from other people outside our immediate family. Others had blessed us with presents that they had picked out just for us so that we would have a happy Christmas.

And that is how we had the best Christmas ever.

Episode Twelve

Stamps of Approval

From the beginning of this trek, the Lord has had me obey His directives without giving me any physical indicator that we could survive at the same time. He gave me no tangible answers to our family, or even our Church leadership, when they asked those "how are you going to????" questions. The answer has most often been, "I don't know. God is just going to have to provide." We got some unexpected financial gifts at the end of December that got us through the first half of January. From that point on, we operated on a budget of zero. People started sending us money. I had no idea of the motives of each giver. Some gave because they wanted to save my wife and children from a fate of starvation due to the haphazard actions of their kooky husband and father. Some were really thrilled about our ministry vision. Some gave because they were excited that someone would literally trust God with their very life. Whatever the motive, we were fed and sheltered.

We did not survive with abundance though. We were perpetually on the verge of financial destruction. Because of the way God had brought us to a point to trust in Him, and then steer us into a stand-alone urban missions ministry on relatively short notice, we did not have conventional support like other American missionaries. Who knew of David Carmichael? Who knew of Educational Christian Ministries? I was not able to ride on the back of a well-known missions organization. What we had to do was actually demonstrate the ministry before we could ever hope to present our vision as viable or credible.

We formed the ministry organization and began teaching in our church as a pilot program in December 1997. By May, 1998, I had taught several classes at my church as a test platform. I was ready to present my program to other churches and ministry organizations. Right about that time, Restoration Church agreed to provide us with regular budgeted support. We began taking our ministry to the impoverished urban communities in our area. Our primary tool is our "Introduction to Computers and Word Processing" course. It provides sixteen hours of computer training, to equip our students with those skills necessary to learn most software applications. Similar training would cost them anywhere from $100.00 to $250.00 but we provide the training for absolutely no charge and we do not solicit for donations. That enables us to minister to a large number of people who do not have access to the training, yet are the ones who need it most.

Throughout 1998, our financial support level was not encouraging but the ministry opportunities were awe-inspiring. I met dozens of people every month that were desperate for the job skill training and for the word of God. Through the medium of the computer classes, I was able to bridge gaps with atheists, Muslims, anti-whites, drug addicts, gang members, prostitutes, homeless, as well as the self-secure middle class. Community leaders, who may have doubted my call at first, began to warm up to my vision. My name began to spread throughout the community in the "East End" of Newport News. God was mightily using me despite what many saw as my cultural disadvantage.

Yet, even with the apparent success of my ministry, we were

discouraged by our state of perpetual poverty. It is true we were being fed, but it was not necessarily nutritious. Every month we had no idea how the mortgage or utilities were going to get paid, or when we would have money for food. On the one hand, it was marvelous how, in the nick of time, someone would bring food or cash. On the other hand, we were humiliated with a sense that we were beggars and freeloaders. Our children did not have ready access to dental care or good clothes. Our vehicles were steadily deteriorating with no hopes of being refurbished. We, by the Lord's providence, had become numbered with "the least of these."

I remember one day walking in to a shelter for the homeless to visit a couple of my students. I became jealous of them as I considered their situation. They had a roof over their heads, a balanced meal waiting for them daily at Saint Paul's Episcopal Church, and they did not have a family depending on them for survival. That is when I realized how low I had stooped. I had wrongfully let myself come to the place of despair. I was despising the place that the Lord had me. I was in sin and I knew it. I knew the word of the Lord that applied. "Be ye content with such things as you have."[40]

By the spring of 1999, our support remained the same as it had been throughout 1998. We had learned to be content with the financial means that God had given us. I was able then to stay focused on the ministry the Lord had called me to. But like the children of Israel in the wilderness journey, I was tempted daily to abandon my confidence in the Lord. I had expected that our financial support would eventually begin to increase. And so I often allowed myself to be distracted by my erroneous expectations. There were other things that began to gnaw on me. There were mixed feelings about me among my church members. I began to hear snide comments. Even worse, I began to hear about discouraging words from our own family members.

Then, I began to experience discouraging moments in my ministry. I was having trouble with a church that was hosting some of our classes. Often times I would commit the entire month to support them. We were told that they were going to conduct their own canvassing for participants and they did not want me interfering. Then

---

[40] *Hebrews 13:5 Let your conduct be without covetousness, and be content with such things as you have. For He Himself has said, "I will never leave you nor forsake you."*

the class day would start and only a small number would show up. We had the capacity for twenty-four people divided into three classes of eight. I had to rush around the community to get enough people signed up to make a training session worth all the expended resources. Part of my discouragement was, even with a decent number of attendees, I seemed to really make a great impact on only a very few people each month. To top it off, our regular support was not sufficient to take care of our basic needs.

One of our most important tasks is to communicate to our supporters and others who have interest. The conventional thought is to communicate to as many people as you can in order to try to motivate offerings. It becomes difficult in discouraging times to write a newsletter that really communicates what God is doing through our ministry. We do not usually see the real work He is doing. We have a sort of tunnel-vision that is distorted by our narrow perspective. The good things we had to report were on a small scale as far as numbers go. God was doing big things to a very small number of people.

So even with the discouragement, I was able to send out a newsletter that had some good reports, and some realistic wishful thinking about what we might be able to do. Although I had written the newsletter, printing it and mailing it is dependent on other things. We did not have enough money to eat, and also buy ink, paper, envelopes and stamps.

As I was printing out the newsletters, I began to grumble in my heart because of a sense of futility I had about that newsletter. When it came time to print the envelopes, I began to grumble some more. I became very aware of how much each letter cost to print, package and send. Once the letters and envelopes were printed, now they needed to be stuffed. I then began to grumble outwardly as I sat on the floor in my office to stuff the envelopes. I complained to the Lord that each letter cost about .90 per person. I whined because I believed people did not really care about my newsletter. In fact, some of them were taking offense because of what I was doing. I started to reason about who I should take off my mailing list. I thought sending anything to them would just be a waste of our meager resources. I also complained because I did not have enough stamps to complete the task and I did not have money to purchase any. Throughout all of this internal and external complaining, I was well aware that my heart was not right and I was in great sin. The thing that helped me was that I was grumbling to the Lord. In doing so, I was subtly pleading for a change of heart, as well as a change of situation.

Episode Twelve

Because I was in a quasi state of prayer, I began to hear the Holy Spirit speaking to me. He told me that I knew I was in sin. The real problem was, I did not believe God would deliver me through all my situations. I had no faith. I was forgetting the mighty works He had done up through that time. God had inspired the list originally. The people I was sending letters to needed to hear what was going on. He reminded me that it was <u>His</u> business to make the ministry fruitful in the way that <u>He</u> decided. I reluctantly confessed my sin and replied to the Lord that I would obey. I would do my work without grumbling. I would trust <u>Him</u> to reap whatever harvest <u>He</u> intended.

I continued my work not very joyfully because I was mourning over my bad attitude. Then, just as I began to press on and stuff my envelopes, my daughter Bethany hesitantly came into my office. She sensed I was not in the best of moods and she did not want to interrupt my work. It seems that the prompting of the Holy Spirit overrode her fears. She apologized for interrupting me, but there was a letter for me that had just been delivered by the postman. I was tempted to be irritated by her interruption. My thought was, "Since when is it an emergency to read the mail?" I caught the obvious bad attitude and reproved myself immediately. I took the letter from her and intended to just set it aside without looking at it. But our

Heavenly Father does speak to His children, and we always hear Him though we often pretend that we do not. His still small voice told me to look at the letter. It was obviously a card like a thank you letter or something. It did not have a return address on it. There was no way for me to preconceive the importance or non-importance of the letter. His still small voice said, "Open it!" I opened the envelope. When I opened the card, what should jump out at me? Stamps!

Humiliation swept over me. God had again showed me that He was not only in charge; He was at work. He was at work before I grumbled. He had the answer to my pleas in the mail before I pled them. There, right on time, were the books of stamps I needed to complete my task. I was ashamed that my attitude was not right when my miracle arrived. I was relieved that I admitted my sin and chosen obedience prior to God showing His tangible presence through the timely gift. After a good cry, I began to experience joy as the revelation of God's mercy cleared my mind of all my prior thoughts. I was able to take pleasure in the task that God had graciously given me to perform. I was assured that my work would be fruitful for God's kingdom, because the King was personally overseeing the operation.

Other than stamps, there was a note encouraging me keep doing the work that God had called me to. A couple of days later, I talked to the person who sent the stamps and I thanked her. To my surprise, she felt embarrassed about her gift. She figured that I would think it strange. She thought money would be a better gift because I could use it for stamps and other needs. I explained the whole story to her and how God had used her gift to speak to me. She told me that she had an internal argument with the Lord over the gift. She sent it in obedience in spite of her natural sense that she ought to be embarrassed. She thanked me for telling her the whole story. My story affirmed to her that God really spoke to her.

The offerings that came as a result of the newsletter were quite meager but God's work over the next class session was powerful. The next class was again poorly marketed. I had to rely on the host church actually contacting people in their community. I anticipated a small turnout, but I had no idea how small. To my dismay, only one person showed up for the first class. I told them that because of the small turnout, I would put off the class for a week to get more people. The second class yielded zero participants. I did not even wait around for the third class. I told the pastor about the situation. I asked him to take the name and telephone number of anybody that showed up, and to tell them to come back the next week. It turned out that the evening class was empty as well. Because of God's encouragement through the stamps, I pressed on without hesitation and started posting notices around the community.

The next week yielded much better results. The noon class was almost full. I taught the class with the appropriate enthusiasm for the ministry I was called to. After that class was over, I waited for the 3:30 class to begin. One person, (D), showed up on time. I asked her to wait about fifteen minutes to see if someone else would show up. I asked her if she could change to fill the last seat in the morning class for the remaining sessions. She agreed. After about thirteen minutes of waiting, another student showed up. I asked her (J) to step into the classroom and to wait for just a few minutes before we would begin. I had frustration gnawing at my soul again. I took a few minutes to go out into the main hallway to pray. I vented my frustration to the Lord and asked Him for relief. His reply, consistent with His nature, was, "You want more? What are you going to do with the two that I gave you?" We both knew the obvious answer to that question. "As you do unto the least of these.., you do it unto me." I knew I had to go teach a computer class to the Lord Jesus.

I asked the new student, (J), if she could come to the evening class the following week. She agreed. I taught the first part of the class, dealing with basic information about the computer components.

Episode Twelve

I then put the two ladies on a ten-minute break and I went to a private room to pray. Usually, after the break, I give a very short sermon about a time when my oldest son fell out of a tree. I always pray first to get in tune with what God intends to do during my message. During my prayer time, the Lord inspired me to teach a different message about the "Prodigal Son." I had never done that one. So, I prayed diligently about what God specifically wanted me to say. He gave me a general idea. I came back after the break and began giving my message. One lady, (D), seemed to act as if she was disgusted with my message and appeared to be deliberately not listening. The other lady, (J), glared at me with anger. I was constantly in prayer as I was giving my eight-minute message. Since it was not a message I had given before, I had to "shoot from the hip." Actually, I was relying on God moment by moment for the next words to say.

Upon concluding my message, the Lord told me to have the ladies lead in the closing prayer. I had to go through the standard, knee-jerk, fleshly questions that are normal for me when God tells me something that does not make natural sense. Of course the first question: "Is that you God? Is that your idea?" In my logical mind, I knew that asking them to lead in prayer, not knowing their spiritual state or background, was not the rational thing to do. I also wondered how they were going to react to the request considering the non-verbal communications they were sending my way during the sermon. Fortunately, I had been in near constant prayer over the previous eighteen minutes. It was fairly easy for me to discern that it was the Lord's prompting. So, I asked them to individually lead in prayer and I told them that I would pray when it was time to end. To my delighted surprise, (D) started to pray. My delight quickly changed to concern as (D) began to openly confess the sin of forsaking God. It occurred to me that I was going to need special discernment to minister to (D). I was initially concerned about how I was going to deal with (D) while hostile (J) was present. Then everything broke loose. Suddenly, (J) burst out crying while (D) was still confessing. Let me tell you, it was a real cloud-burst. She was crying in spasms. Soon, (D) had to end her prayer because the sound of it was conflicting with the loud anguish coming out of (J). Both (D) and I stayed silent while (J) continued to wail. I prayed in earnest like I had never prayed before. I begged God to show me what to do. He was obviously at work. I did not want to mess it up by saying something just to feel like I was doing the "minister" thing. So I continued to pray for myself, (D), and (J).

(J) started to settle down a bit. I spoke, "(J)? What is God doing with you right now?" That began a forty-minute session of continual confession of sin and a story of desperation. (J) awoke alongside of a man she had only met that early morning. She was disgusted with herself and the lifestyle that had brought her to that situation. When she left being with that stranger, she just walked down the street lamenting her life. She was questioning why she should not end her life. She did not know whether she was talking to herself or talking to God. As (J) was walking, she looked up and saw our sign advertising the free class starting in only a few minutes. She determined, to either herself or God, whoever it was that she was talking to, that she would just try one last thing. She would try to do one good thing for herself to see if it would make a difference, to see if going on with life was worth it. She walked directly from where the sign was to our class and came in late. I told (J) that what she needed was forgiveness. She said that she knew it. Her friends kept telling her she needed to forgive herself. She said, "I know I need to forgive myself but I just can't seem to really do it."

What (J) was experiencing was the guilt of sin. She recognized the destruction that sin was wreaking on her life but she was not able to pull herself out of its downward spiral. She could not escape the feeling of being guilty despite her futile attempts to "forgive herself." I do not know whether what I said next was wisdom from God or just completely obvious to my mind. I realized that what I was about to say would come out sounding fairly offensive, but I knew it needed to be said. I said rather strongly, "Who are you to forgive yourself?" Her eyes changed from a look of sorrow to one of shock. Her jaw literally dropped open. It was not the counsel she expected to hear and it was certainly not what she wanted to hear. I just removed what she thought was her only possible lifeline. It was readily understandable that if she was not able to forgive herself, she had no hope to ever recover her life. I said it again very strongly, "Who are you to forgive yourself? You are not a good person. You said yourself that your life is steeped in sin. What right do you have to forgive yourself. If you did forgive yourself, what good would it do you? Your forgiveness is not worth anything." What I said was very shocking to someone who can only see herself in a corrupt state. She understood, however, that what I said was horribly true. Her forgiveness of herself was valueless. The room became silent. She dropped her head. She seemed to have no hope.

Because of the silence, I was able to speak quietly though my words sounded loud. I said, "(J), what you need to do is **receive** the forgiveness that our Holy God has already prepared for you." She looked up into my eyes and received those words like her soul was a dry sponge soaking up living water. I explained to her that Jesus was the perfect Lamb of God who was without sin. His forgiveness is the only satisfactory forgiveness because <u>He</u> is worthy of the glory of God. His blood was spilled to completely cover her sin. It would cover her sin if she would acknowledge Jesus as her Lord, and Savior, and receive the eternal life that He has offered to her. If she would receive Jesus Christ as Lord and Savior, forgiveness would come as a result.

Truth swept into her mind. The Lord showed Himself to (J) right there in front of (D) and me. She began to weep in a different way than she had before. It was a sobbing that communicated a sense of relief and release. She began to let go of her sin and give it over to God. She experienced God's forgiveness. (J) began to spontaneously confess to the Lord, not her sin, but her sinful state. She asked Christ to be the Lord of every part of her life. She started to say in her prayer that she would forgive herself and then she corrected herself as God gave her understanding. She acknowledged that she was forgiven. She thanked God for what He had done for her, and for what He was doing for her at that moment. (J) did not need to be 'led' in "The sinners prayer." Her prayer was spontaneous and true.

We never did get back to teaching computer stuff after the break and sermon. We just met with the Living God. Our evening class was a nice size and we continued the course with only a noon and evening class from that point forward. The pastor contacted (J) and he began counseling sessions with her. It was a very productive class from that point onward.

Throughout that course, we still had very meager support. Even with God showing that He was obviously at work, I still would fret about whether my efforts were futile. I took our meager, and what I saw as inadequate, sustenance as a message that God was not blessing our ministry. I even whined about the costs of printing certificates and reference letters at the end of the course. Of course God showed me again that my heart was not right and that I had better correct my attitude.

When the course was completed, the pastor presented graduation certificates to each student in a very festive atmosphere. He gave an opportunity for the students to tell what they got out of the course. Every student had a powerful testimony. I wrote some of them down, after-the-fact, to encourage people through our next newsletter:

"DP" - I experienced a literal spiritual attack discouraging me from completing the course. I had flashbacks to the times I had experienced humiliation when I failed in academics. I remembered the scriptures you told us in class and I began to pray and a claim those scriptures. I began to feel a peace from God that released me from fear and I came to class (test day) with confidence that I had never felt before. I was a little nervous, but I did well and I really know and experienced that I can do all things through Christ who strengthens me.

"J" - I had to fight to get here on the first day. Everything in my life was falling apart and I knew I had to do something positive for myself. When I got here, brother David began to speak about the prodigal son and I knew it was God speaking right to me. I really experienced God's forgiveness for the first time in my life. I knew I was a child of God and my Father did not want me living like I was. I just confessed my sin to God right there in the classroom and brother David and sister "D" just ministered to me. Since that day my life has totally changed. I have had victory in so many areas I cannot begin to tell you. I thank God for Brother David and his ministry.

"M" - Before I came to this course, I was a very bitter person. I was unhappy and I was somebody nobody wanted to be around. Ask my cousin ("W" nods her head in agreement). But since I have come to this course, I have changed ("W" nods her head again). God has really used the preaching of the word during counsel time to get me to change my attitude. Now I'm happy, I think about others first, and I know the Lord has used this to change me and make me the way he wants me to be.

"W" - I have to say the same thing as ("D"). I had come to a point where I thought it just wasn't worth trying to improve myself. I mean what's the use. I'm over forty and I didn't see myself as being able to really change my situation. But now I know I can do anything that I want to do with the Lord's help. This class was hard, but I did it. And it's going to help me to teach myself to do other things. I've decided I'm going to school and I'm signed up for classes this fall (round of cheers and applause from the students).

After congratulating the students and sending them on their way, I packed up my stuff and headed for home. All of the things that I had wrestled with God about over the previous two months came to my mind. I remembered the stamps showing up at just the right time. I remembered God questioning me about whether I was willing to be faithful with the little He gave me. Then I thought about all the mighty works I had seen Him do in the lives of the students over those last several weeks. I felt God giving me a spirit of liberty and I began to worship Him with tears of joy. I had to slow down and pull over on the highway on-ramp for a minute because I was not able to drive in my intensely emotional state.

God showed His glory again. He did His work, <u>His</u> way, and He let me in on it.

Episode Thirteen

Classroom Claims

God does not measure success by statistical analysis. I, on the other hand, tend to use my definitions of success to confirm whether God's blessing is on whatever I am doing. There are some spiritual precepts that I rightfully grasp onto to justify my analysis. I am supposed to judge a tree by its fruit. "A good tree cannot bear bad fruit."[41] "...indeed bears good fruit and produces: Some a hundred fold, some sixty and some thirty."[42] However, I rarely can predict the

---

[41] *Matthew 7:18a*
[42] *Matthew 13:23b*

outcome of the work God assigns to me. In most cases, things look dismal at first. If things looked more promising, I might have a tendency to trust in myself rather than God. Just as the scripture says, "Faith without works is dead.", I believe, 'A work not of faith is dead.'

I naturally tend to measure success by analysis of a work that has affected something that is measurable. I do not see things as God sees them. God's view of His orchard is from an overhead perspective rather than from in the weeds. God is a strategist and tactician. He sees each activity as it effects His entire scheme. If I get frustrated with the seemingly insignificant tasks He gives me, it is because I am deceived into thinking that there are bigger and better things I should be doing to fulfill God's mission. I do not understand that the little part He has given me will have a powerful, and often miraculous, effect. Especially when it is combined with other works He is doing elsewhere.

As you read the remainder of this chapter, you will see the words: I, me & my. In a ministry newsletter, I would normally use words like: we, us & our. "My" ministry is really "our" ministry. I might be the one carrying on the workload, but "we" are actually the ministers. "We" being those who have supported my family and me to enable us to fulfill the command of God and actually eat at the same time. Each person that gives a gift of faith to us boosts my faith. It is fuel for the spiritual fire I need to make a lasting impact on other's lives. I have used the words I, me & my, for the remainder of the chapter for the sake of technical accuracy and not to assume any credit. The only thing that "I" can boast is that God has done a mighty work and He has let "me" participate in it.

Over these years of ministry, I have most often carried out my tasking without expending too much energy measuring success. I have focused mostly on seeking ministry opportunities that are within the Lord's will rather than my own schemes. I have been thrilled with opportunities to provide a vibrant ministry to those who need it most, even if it is not appreciated. For the most part, I have been satisfied knowing I was doing what God told me to do. Then, when I least expect it, God shows his glory through marvelous works, right before my very eyes.

Because of my physical limitations, I do not have means to keep track of the long-term effects of my ministry upon the students' lives. I do get small glimpses, usually from hearsay reports. One day, God miraculously gave me access to a live testimonial to give to someone who asked about the success of "my" ministry.

Episode thirteen

On March 13, 2001, I took my son, Jesse, to his soccer practice at a local middle school athletic field. I was visiting with one of the other parents, Katherine, who is an extremely well qualified computer operations instructor. She asked me how my computer-training ministry was going. I told her about the training sites, our student demographics, and some success stories about students who were employed as a direct result of our training.

Katherine asked me if I had any stories about the effects of our sermons. I gave her a few examples. Just as I finished my stories, I looked down the length of the running track that surrounds the soccer field. I saw a lady who had graduated one of our classes about a year-and-a-half earlier. She was power-walking with a young lady who turned out to be her daughter. She had finished her normal number of laps when her daughter talked her into doing another lap. Otherwise, I would not have seen her.

As I spotted my alumnus, I said to Katherine, "Hey! Don't listen to me; let's find out from somebody who has been through one of the classes. There's one right now!" After my student closed in about ten paces, I walked out in front of her with a memory-challenged look on my face. I said, "I can't remember your first name but your last name is Farrior." She smiled an embarrassed but big smile and said, "It's

Phyllis. How are you?" I shortened our re-acquaintance because I wanted to interview her while I still had Katherine as an audience. I knew the soccer practice would end very shortly and she had a very close schedule.

I told Phyllis about Katherine's questions and I pointed out the timeliness of her arrival. I asked Phyllis to answer some questions so Katherine could get a good understanding of our ministry. I interviewed Phyllis to see if she had a special story. Her response was overwhelming. She told us a story of the great discouragement she had experienced leading up to our course. She was in her forties and had been displaced out of her job because of cutbacks and reorganization. When she tried to find employment, her lack of computer skills kept her from being considered. Teenagers out of high school were getting jobs and she was being excluded. She had a new computer but she had no idea how to operate it. Her children knew how to use it but they did not have the ability to teach her. They were not able to override her increasing insecurity and fear of failure.

One day, Phyllis saw our brochure telling of free computer training. She had to admit that her despair gave her no excuse to miss out on an opportunity to learn marketable skills. She signed up for the class but did not really think it would make a significant change in her life.

I remembered that Phyllis had done very well in the course. However, after the training, she did not really think she would be able to compete in the job market. Never-the-less, Phyllis decided to apply for a job at a local telemarketing company. She wanted to see if her knew skills would make a difference. To her surprise and delight, she found out that she excelled compared to her young, more experience, competition. She was able to teach her coworkers many things. She was rapidly promoted within her sphere. Phyllis regained her confidence. She ventured out to another job that provided better pay and benefits, among other things.

I could see the hunger for more growth in Phyllis' eyes. She told us, "You should see me now! You can't get me off of that thing. Ask my daughter." (Daughter nods earnestly) Phyllis told us how she poured herself into learning every application she could get her hands on. By what she said, she certainly surpassed my knowledge of operating some of the same programs. There was a particular certification that Phyllis had conquered. Katherine understood what it was but I did not. As icing on the cake, Phyllis said that only a few days before, she had been accepted for a particular position. She had been chosen over many other applicants. The position started at twenty-five dollars per hour and was one that was very prestigious, requiring a superb knowledge of many program applications. Katherine was very familiar with the company and the particular position. The two ladies had a mini-conversation of their own since they were the only ones in our group who knew what they were talking about. Katherine was visibly impressed by Phyllis' accomplishments. It was obvious to Katherine that our computer training had a vital impact on Phyllis. It had been used mightily to equip Phyllis for success and livelihood.

Since Katherine was captivated, I took the opportunity to fish for a spiritual success story. I asked Phyllis if any of the mini-sermons had made an impact on her life. Her facial expressions and body language told us much when she suddenly assumed a look of reverent fear. She sandwiched her face with the palms of her hands and gasped, "Yeeessss!" Phyllis emphatically said there was one message that was exactly about what she was going through during that time.

Phyllis retold the story that she heard, in a condensed version and in the correct sequence, telling us the story-line and key teaching points. The message motivated her to reverse a self-destructive path. She began to conform to what she knew God wanted of her. After her repentance in response to the message, Phyllis started enjoying the fruit of God's blessings and was still experiencing them. She began walking steadfastly with the Lord and became actively involved with, and committed to, her church. She was extremely grateful for the change in her life and the impact it was having on her children. They were not only being well provided for physically, they were being well fed and trained spiritually. There was no doubt by Phyllis's testimony that our ministry was just what she needed, when she needed it. I believe the timing of our meeting that day was arranged by divine appointment.

I take every opportunity I can to show what God is doing in the way of Divine miraculous intervention. It encourages people to seek a deeper personal relationship with our Living God through the person of Jesus and the Holy Spirit. In Phyllis's story, we saw the tangible physical and spiritual benefit to our student. Our little meeting encouraged Katherine and me. Phyllis was reminded of how much God loves her and that He did a miraculous work in her life.

I have heard other stories where people have benefitted physically through our ministry. That is expected since meeting physical needs is one of our primary goals. But the number of people helped physically is still not our measure of success. I have had some interesting experiences relating to the spiritual aspect of our ministry that give indications of its vibrancy.

I have periodically set aside a class entirely for the participants of a ministry called Youth Challenge. Youth Challenge is a ministry targeted to those who have been involved in drug abuse. It is a spiritual program whose design is to free people from their drug addiction by the power of God. There are three major phases to the program. The first few months have the participants in a rigorous program that only a staff person or participant can describe to you. Then they spend several more months in a place they call "The Mountain." There, on a farm, they continue their spiritual and work ethic training. Finally, some are allowed to return to the first ministry site as an intern. The interns on several occasions have been allowed to participate in our training the last month before they finish their internship.

On the first day of one Youth Challenge class, I met a class of six students consisting of three men and three women. I spent the first hour, as usual, teaching them about computer hardware. It was quite exciting teaching them because they were all very hungry to learn. They knew how much the information would benefit them. The close of the first hour came and it was time to take a ten-minute break before I came back to give my mini-sermon.

Episode thirteen

I have about half-a-dozen preplanned messages that I use to systematically share the gospel of Jesus Christ. It dawned on me before the class started that my standard opening sermon would not hold this group's attention. It is a captivating story but they, through their program, are overly used to hearing little sermons. The theme was something that they had been subjected to daily for the last six months. I was tempted to just stick to my rote. I thought that I could probably be suave enough to at least make it entertaining. I concluded though, it would just be a dead work. I needed a message empowered by God. So, when I went off to pray as I usually do during the ten-minute break, I complained to the Lord about my dilemma.

I went to a dusty unused room in the hundred-year-old building at Zoe Community Church. I lay headlong and face-down. I earnestly prayed to the Lord, "Lord? You know these guys hear sermons everyday. I don't want this to be just another sermon. I need a word from You! I need to get a word from you that cuts straight to their hearts...." Suddenly, while I was still mentally and physically voicing my supplication, my thoughts were strongly interrupted with "Annanias and Saphira!"

I paused in my prayer. I shut down my thinking and listened with my spirit. I did not sense anything else. So I prayed, "Annanias and Saphira?" In my spirit, I did not sense that it was of my flesh. Instead, I knew somehow that it was right on target. I continued to pray, "What do you want me to say about Annanias and Saphira?" I sensed nothing else from the Lord about the subject. So, I did the silly thing that I usually do. I started using my finite mind to come up with a groovy message about the subject. As soon as I started thinking of a something to say, I felt a huge burden of guilt. I recognized right away that God often uses that guilt feeling to show me what I am not supposed to do. I was bewildered. I prayed, "Lord? You want me to just say Annanias and Saphira?" I sensed peace in my spirit and the power of God settling upon me. Even after that, I tried to shrug off the sense of God's anointing and try to think of something to say about Annanias and Saphira. I did not want to look like a knucklehead to my sermon-seasoned audience. The more I tried to think of a teaching point, the more I was disturbed in my spirit. I was figuratively buckin' and snortin' in my spirit. I voiced rhetorically to the Lord; "You just want me to say - Annanias and Saphira? With no message?" I sensed the affirmation of the Lord. I knew that any work I did in the flesh to produce a sermon would be totally contrary to God's will.

Episode thirteen

Here I was, earnestly asking God to give me a word. Then, when He gives me a word, I desperately fight against it. I was too chicken to do something that would seem crazy to my listeners. I complained to the Lord then, not about my need for a word with power, but instead for some kind of relief from His tasking so that I would not have to risk humiliation. God did not give me relief. I knew what I had to do. I knew God's will. He wanted me to just walk in and say (obviously when they were all paying attention) "Annanias and Saphira". So, I prayed; "Okay Lord. I will go in and say Annanias and Saphira without a message to go with it."

What I actually did was not an act of faith or of obedience. Nonetheless, God was faithful and showed His power despite my unbelief. I acted much like Moses did when God told Him to speak to the rock. Moses, instead of doing exactly what God told him, and no more, did what his flesh urged him to do. He struck the rock twice rather than speaking to it. He suffered the displeasure of the Lord. His audience did benefit from the miracle by enjoying the fresh water and the glory of the Lord. Moses, on the other hand, missed out on two blessings. He was not able to enjoy the moment, and he missed out on a future blessing.[43] Because of my unbelief and fear, I did not do exactly what God told me to do.

I walked into the room to find all the students ready for a message. However, instead of abruptly declaring "Annanias and Saphira", I began to speak other words. The words had nothing to do with a teaching point on the subject, but I was not being obedient to carry out God's directive. What I said was a reasonable lead-in. I said, "Since you guys get preached to every day, I asked God to give me a specific word." I paused. I sensed the displeasure of the Lord and wondered if He was still willing to use me. All the students looked at me in anticipation. Then I said abruptly, "Annanias and Saphira!" Upon the speaking of the word, in spite of my interference, God manifested His supernatural work.

At the conclusion of my statement, two ladies sitting together on my left both doubled over as if they had been punched in the stomach. They both appeared to be gasping for breath. They turned toward each other with looks of terror on their faces and began an intense parley. Their conversation was loud enough to disturb the class but hushed enough that we could not understand the words they were

---

[43] *Numbers 20:7-12*

saying. It made the rest of us uncomfortable. By their physical and emotional reactions, it was apparent that I had actually gotten a word from God. The word was designed for those two ladies. The rest of the group tried to distract themselves from the commotion across the room. The third woman in the group sat silently and the three young men started jovial small talk to break the tension.

One of the young men said, "I know that story. That's the one about..." What he described was the wrong story. One of his classmates told him that he was wrong. However, when the second man tried to correct his friend, he started describing the wrong story as well. Although God had not allowed me to formulate a sermon, He gave me an opportunity to tell the story and it's application.

I began to tell the young men about who Annanias and Saphira were. As I went through the various aspects of the story, the two distraught ladies uncontrollably winced and groaned. Their reaction was by reflex that was too strong to be subdued. Their reactions became increasingly violent as the story progressed. I gathered by observation, as the ladies clutched one another, the theme of their conversation was essentially, 'what shall we do?'. By the time I concluded the story with a short summary, the ladies were trying to recover their wits, emotions and breathing.

Through my interaction with them over the next few weeks, I came to understand that the two ladies took care of whatever problem had been exposed. God had blessed them through His mighty miracle. I was happy to know God was patient with me and would use me despite my unbelief and unwillingness to obey Him whole-heartedly. Watching God work in those ladies lives was exciting and rewarding in itself. Like Moses though, I may have missed out on a huge blessing that the Lord had otherwise planned for me. I am assured, however, that God has His hand on my life.

The numbers of times God performs miracles in the classroom, though thrilling and encouraging, is also not a measure of success. Keeping statistics of spiritual manifestations is not a realistic endeavor. The measure of success must be - whether or not I have dutifully carried out the specific directives of our Commander.

It is obvious to me that God was doing an active work in the lives of the two ladies whom He spoke to in the class. The staff at Youth Challenge had been obedient to the Lord's bidding and God was diligently working through them. By the context of the word God gave me to say, I can gather that the two ladies had agreed to hide something. The Holy Spirit had most likely challenged them previously. Then God used me as His mouthpiece in order to finish the work that He had begun elsewhere. God probably would have used some other means to challenge their sinful act even if I had not fulfilled my part. However, I would have missed out on an opportunity to be used and to see the God's glory. Also, the two ladies would have been at greater risk of hardening their hearts as time wore on. Any refusal to speak the word that God gave me would have set them up for a greater fall.

This is a story of success because it shows that God is at work in this ministry. It is not measurable though. I cannot make a cost-versus-benefit calculation. I am looking at God's field from within the weeds where I cannot see the extent of the harvest. I have no idea what mighty works God intends to perform in, and through, the lives of those two ladies. Who knows? Maybe they will tell someone the story how God miraculously called down their sin. Maybe that someone will be a famous and effective evangelist someday.

When I judge the worth of my life calling, and my current assignment, I erroneously begin to count numbers of people attending classes. A Large class of students is not necessarily a good thing. It provides a nice healthy statistic for a cost-versus-benefit analysis, but it does not mean that God is actually at work. The many distractions of a large class often preclude me from being able to effectively minister to the students' spiritual needs.

When I see God do a supernatural work in the life of a student, I cannot equate it as a measure of "my" success. It is a work of God. Though they might encourage our supporters, the supernatural works that God does are often too holy, or too confidential, to put into a public report. Our measure of success must be: "Are we seeking God's face? Is He giving us specific direction? Are we carrying out His directives?" Once we begin obeying God's directives, the results are at His pleasure.

Episode Fourteen

Presuming Upon God
Part I

Often people make the assertion that the opposite of faith is fear. Fear is arresting, whereas faith is liberating. From the beginning, our greatest fear was the challenge to our survival. God was requiring us to work for Him, with no specific contract, or promise of a certain paycheck. There is an earthly price tag on life. Other inhabitants of this planet demand money or they will not allow you to have food, shelter or liberty. The work we were called to do did not produce food or money. Obedience to God put us in a position that if He did not come through daily, we were sunk. Fortunately, God has been extremely faithful to deliver sustenance to us, often using timeliness to demonstrate His glory.

In the last part of 1988, we attended a seminar about how to manage your money. We started putting our money in envelopes for each budgeted item. Whenever we considered buying something, we checked the appropriate envelope and determined whether or not it was something we were able to purchase. We knew exactly how much money would be available every month. When we conserved, we saw tangible results. We left anything extra, at the end of the month, in the envelopes. We were generally prepared for months that had greater demands in any spending area. It became easy to save money for vacations, to limit our expenditures on extravagant things, have money to give gifts to others, and still not fall short in a critical area. To make this all possible, I was making a fairly decent wage as a Chief Petty Officer.

When we started working for God, there was no income from which to base a budget plan. Our costs were increasing with the number and physical maturity of our children. We had new expenses to carry out the ministry operations. Also, we had no way of knowing when we would actually receive money. The envelope system could not be justified. When we had a need, such as food, the phone bill would just have to wait. There was no such thing as a surplus, only a need and subsequent provision.

'In the beginning', my wife would regularly approach me with trepidation to ask, do we have money for....? 'In the beginning', I would be quite frustrated by the question. With the little money we had, which was always less than our need, how was I expected to reserve money for any particular item? All I could do was consider the need and then look into the till to see if the money was there. I would ask my wife, "Is it a need?" Again, 'in the beginning', she would get frustrated with my question as well. She thought our spending decisions were based upon the stack of bills in the "in box." She nearly always answered yes and then explained why it was a need. I would give her the money she requested if there was any available at all. Had we a regular paycheck that told us our total spending power, I would have been making decisions the way that she expected. What I was actually doing was, 'not worrying about tomorrow because today had enough cares of it's own.' Managing money in that way is very easy. When money comes in, it usually has a place to go other than an envelope. If we need food, we buy food and let the electric bill wait. Eventually, money will come in to take care of the electricity.

During these years my Pastor would ask me, "How are you doing financially?" I never got over being dumbfounded by that question every time I hear it. I have no idea how I am doing financially. Actually, I am not doing financially. You can only know how you are doing financially if you know your income and expenses. I know neither of them. If I did know my financial situation, what could I do about it anyway? I can guess our minimum requirements if someone really wants to know them and then all I can do is presume God will come through on time. The alternative is to abandon the ministry and scramble about trying to find ways to make money.

God has been very faithful to let others know how I am doing financially. He has stirred in other people's hearts a desire to give to us. We have not had to beg for the money that we receive. When we do start begging, the money seems to dry up. When we get involved in our finances, we start to reap the penalty of not believing God for our salvation. When we let go of our schemes to save ourselves, His blessings begin to flow.

On one day, we did not even have enough loose change to buy a can of frozen orange juice. We had food in the refrigerator and the pantry that maintained us meagerly. We subsisted for a significant part on large quantities of bread that people brought to us. Things were very tight. We were a bit discouraged by what our eyes could see, but we pressed on with the calling that God had placed upon us.

One day, my wife wanted to make some coffee for me to enjoy while I worked. She also wanted to make some sweet-tea for her and the children. When Leslie opened the cabinet door, she found that there were no coffee filters, and no sugar. Though tempted to despair, she took it to the Lord in prayer. Leslie's prayer complained about the situation, saying that it would be nice to be able to enjoy something to drink besides water. Leslie admitted to the Lord in her prayer that coffee filters and sugar were something that she could live without. Never-the-less, she asked the Lord to give us coffee filters and sugar. Les put it out of her mind and went about her day, not telling me about it.

Later that day, Les got a call from a friend who said she had some things her son left in his apartment that he just moved out of. She had prayed to the Lord to tell her whom she should give it to. The Lord put us in her mind and she wanted to bring the things to us. When she arrived and opened the hatchback of her car, Leslie looked into the box that contained the items. There was a huge stack of coffee filters, bags of sugar (some had been previously opened), and an oil lantern.

I am sure that we would give credit to God if someone had

dropped off a box of groceries that just happened to include coffee filters and sugar. I am sure that God would have deserved the credit. But this boxed delivery, by it's limitations, showed us that God is at work continually, that He knows our need, and He is really listening to our prayers. Because of all the circumstances surrounding the event, I must conclude that the lantern was not just random junk that came our way. The lantern made the event a teachable moment for me. God's desire is for us to trust Him completely rather than trying to see too far ahead in our journey. We know the scripture, "Your word is a lamp unto my feet and a light to my path."[44] On a dark night in the woods, an oil lamp unto our feet is only able to illuminate a short pace ahead of us. The darkness of night, and the uncertainty of the path, requires us to focus on each step. If our concentration on each step is not keen, there is a high probability of stumbling on a rock, root, or divot. I saw that God wants me to worry only about each day, one step at a time. I have no idea which way the path will twist and turn. All I know is that God will illumine the way to lead me safely to my eventual destination.

There are many other Divine interventions that have sustained us

---

[44] *Psalm 119:105*

over these years. One was particularly educational. We were just like the children of Israel, whining because we forgot the goodness of God and the miracles He had previously performed. In December, 2000, we carried out tasks, sometimes, by faith, satisfied in them and often, without faith, complaining through them. Christmas approached and God had not placed in our budget envelope (figuratively speaking) any money to purchase Christmas presents. He did however provide Grandparents for our children who sent us money so that we could bless the kids. We, as parents, have a desire to give our children good gifts. We want to be able to have the means to bless them physically as well as spiritually. This particular Christmas however, we did not have the means to do it. All the money that came in went to things that were needed for our survival, with nothing left over.

One Saturday, my wife and I went to Sam's Club to spend the Grandparent's money on our children. We had mixed feelings as we approached our day of shopping. We were grateful that we had something to buy presents for our children with but we felt guilty that we had nothing with which to buy something for their grandparents. Before we got out of our decrepit van in the Sam's Club parking lot, my wife began to vent her feelings.

Usually, I think and feel similar things that my wife thinks and feels about stressful situations. I normally deal with them internally. I force myself to come to the logical spiritual conclusion and resolution in my mind. Only then do I act on it. My wife needs to vent all her feelings before ever coming close to resolving an issue in her mind. There is one major problem. If I have thought about something and have chosen a particular quasi-spiritual conclusion, I go a bit crazy when my wife starts her venting process. She says what she feels even though she is not committed to holding on to the feeling. She is actually trying to get rid of the feeling. She is the one of us that speaks the problem. I normally don't speak until I am able to speak the solution. Thus, we come into conflict with each other. Her venting seems to me as if she is cursing God. My confession of God's provision, in spite of the lack of it being present, seems to her as if I am ignoring the problem. So, on Saturday, December 16, 2000, why wife and I were having a very unhappy and loud (discussion) in our van at Sam's Club in Newport News.

Because of my wife's frustration, she began to complain. I, in my quasi-spiritual way, was telling her that we needed to trust God and not complain. She accused me of being outside of God's will and hiding under a cloak of ministry. I considered it a very irrational low blow. I started citing Biblical principles we are supposed to believe. I

229

hoped that she would withdraw her accusation and be encouraged. We had a pretty thorough and brutal bash at one another in our mutual self-righteousness. My wife had finally done enough venting to say something, in her right-reason, that hit me right between the eyes. She pointed out that our car did not run because there was a hole in the engine. Our van was constantly breaking down and was not a safe vehicle for a mother to have to be taking her children around town in. Leslie pointed out that our refrigerator door was warped and the compressor was about to give out completely. She said that if God had truly willed our ministry, He would provide for our needs. She said a decent vehicle and a functional refrigerator were essential needs. I had to agree with her.

I challenged her to voice her request just like she had about the computer we needed and the coffee filters and sugar. I told her to describe her need for a vehicle. We needed something that was close to new, in good running condition, and safe. It needed to carry us all and be something that would allow us to take long trips to visit family members. She wanted it to have a good sound system. It needed to play cassette tapes or CDs for the kids on long trips. It must have controls in the front that would be able to make adjustments between the front and back sound volume. We needed something that could also haul my computers around from class to class. We <u>presumed</u> it had to be a full-size van so it would meet the people comfort requirements and the power and space requirements for computer transport.

The next concern was the refrigerator. She wanted a large capacity, side-by-side, almond colored refrigerator with an ice and water dispenser in the door, and glass shelves. That was it. We settled our argument and had an earnest prayer session together there in the parking lot at Sam's Club.

As we came to a resolution of our problem, a sense of faith, peace, joy and (very importantly) love began to return to our hearts. We started to cry as we fully remembered all the blessings we received from God over the most recent years. We admitted our pettiness and lack of faith. We recalled the Christmas only three years before when we were much worse off financially. God poured a blessing on us that we could never imagine. Well, we finally stepped into Sam's Club and spent our parent's money on the kids. It was satisfying. We knew the kids would really enjoy the presents and the grandparents would be satisfied with the items we purchased.

One of the presents we wanted to purchase was a snare drum so our oldest son Jesse could learn to play. We did not have the money for it until two days later. Leslie and I drove to AL&M music store in Norfolk, Virginia. We were talking about the blessings of God and how grateful we were to be able to buy our son a snare drum. When we stopped at a very busy intersection, suddenly, the transmission stopped working. The van would not go forward or backward. Another motorist stepped out of his car and helped me push the van into a muffler shop parking lot on the corner of the intersection.

The resolution to our beautiful argument, two days before, had brought us to the point that we were able to trust God. We were not frustrated by the incident; we were relieved by it. We knew that God would provide us with another vehicle because that is what we needed. The van was dead. The transmission going out on the van was the straw that broke the camel's back. Leslie and I had a wake for it right there in the muffler shop parking lot. God had given us a pretty strong dose of faith. We were filled with overwhelming joy thinking about how God was going to bless us. We sat down on the curb at the edge of the parking lot and started thanking God for what He was going to do. These were not magic words that some might try to put into a formula. This thanksgiving experience was stirred up by the Holy Spirit. We were acting out what some might call the "name it and claim it" motif, but it was not because of a calculated formula. It was the natural thing to do.

I had been telling myself I was trusting God, but I did not trust Him enough to actually ask Him to meet my specific need. In this situation, my wife forced me to face facts. Since a good vehicle was an obvious need, I had to either ask God for it or come up with my own scheme to acquire it. When the van died, our need became even greater. We were now completely stranded. Since our need had increased, I sensed more intensely that God was going to do a miraculous work to solve our problem.

I truly believed God for a miracle because God had stirred up faith in my heart. Rather than worry about the van, we told the proprietor of the muffler shop that we would be back soon with a tow truck. Then we walked about a mile down Military Highway to the music store to purchase the snare drum. I had an interesting experience on the way. I learned that I can be wrongly presumptuous about the work God is doing and yet still be in His will. God has been faithful to do His work even though our faith is flawed.

While we walked down the road, I was excited about the prospect of getting a new vehicle. I had no idea how it would happen but I knew that God was going to show off. I started looking around for a vehicle that God might give us. I would not be surprized if somebody just drove up and gave us one. As we were walking, we came across a car rental place that also sold cars. There was a fifteen-passenger van for sale and we gave it a good looking over. Then I saw a green customized Dodge van. This is where presumption kicked in, though God used it anyway.

We opened the van and looked inside. Let's face it, it was beautiful, being that it was a customized van. There was no price on it, so I went to ask the lot owner about it. I told him my situation. I asked him flat out if he would be willing to give it to me. I had no idea how God was going to meet our need so I just "asked". He said he could not do it but said he would be willing to sell it to me for what he owed the bank, $15,000.00. I had a hint of disappointment that the miracle did not happen right then and there. But still, $15,000.00 was a really good deal for that van. So, now we just had to come up with $15,000.00.

God had not told me to buy that particular van. But I was full of the zeal of the Lord. The van that I saw would suit me quite well, and I was in the mood for a miracle. So I set my sights on that van. I will tell you without hesitation that setting my sights on that van was a work of the flesh. At the time I did not know it. I was beginning to get a bit uppity in my faith. I was lusting after God's blessing. My problem was, I had never been in a situation just like this one. God was going to bless me but I did not know how. God had miraculously worked to give me a house in 1988. He had stirred up in our hearts a desire for the particular house before we knew He was going to perform a miracle. In this instance, we knew the miracle was coming but we did not know how to act in the meantime.

After asking the owner about the van, I turned to go back toward it where Les was waiting. On the way I had a thought that was definitely stirred up by the Lord. I needed to tithe His gift! "How do I tithe a van? Do I take off a wheel and give it away? Do I come up with money equivalent to ten percent of the vehicle's value?" So I asked, "Lord; how do I tithe a van?" The answer came immediately. I cannot quote words from the Lord in this particular situation, but the Holy Spirit gave me understanding. 'I had to come up with $1,500.00 to give away. The Lord is Jehovah Jireh, "the Lord is provider." Just as He provided the sacrifice for Abraham, He would also provide in this instance for me.' God did not give me a word about the particular van but He did give me a word about this offering I was supposed to give prior to receiving a van. The $1,500.00 would be a faith gift. It was not something that I was bartering with the Lord over, "I will give you $1,500.00 and you give me

$15,000.00 worth of vehicle." It really was a spiritual understanding that He gave me. I also understood that getting the $1,500.00 would be a miracle. I had no means by which to acquire it. So, until I got $1,500.00 to give away, my van hopes were on hold.

We purchased Jesse's snare drum and telephoned Kessler's Towing in Hampton. Fred and Bonnie Everett lent their Volkswagen van to us until our miracle showed up. We did nothing else from that point but wait for Christmas to show up.

On Sunday morning of our Christmas service, I opened the church at about 7:15 to pray and get ready to lead the worship service. As I approached the door, the Lord very clearly spoke to me. "Tithe the tithe as a first-fruit offering." I stopped and did the standard comprehension check. "Is that you Lord?" I sensed in my spirit that it was the Lord who spoke to me. I understood right away what He was saying. However, just like the other amounts of money, I did not have $150.00 either. I started questioning in my mind how I was going to come up with $150.00. I had planned to give our broken car away but now I thought I would have to sell it to raise the money. I figured I could get $150.00 for the car since it was a Mustang and could be sold for parts. Immediately I got what some call a "check in my spirit." It is like a twinge of guilt. I knew that it was the wrong thing to do and that it would displease God. Selling the mustang seemed reasonable since I did not have any other means, and I owned the silly car. I should be able to change my mind regarding what I wanted to do with it. Well, sell the car or not, it did not matter. I would still give the car away, but I knew that I was supposed to come up with 150.00. I was to give it away as a first-fruit offering for the $1,500.00 God would give me to give away for a tithe of the $15,000.00 worth of vehicle I was going to get.

At the end of the service, one of the elders came forward with some envelopes. I had completely forgotten that they give each of the staff members a gift at Christmas time. I was called forward, given my envelope and an embrace. I took my envelope and sat back down. We sang the closing anthem and people began to leave. I opened my envelope and what was in it? A check for $150.00. Boy was I excited. I rushed to the first person I could get to. I flashed the check in front of him and exuberantly exclaimed "God's going to perform a miracle." I told him how just five hours earlier I had gotten a word from the Lord to give away $150.00. I did not have $150.00 when God told me, but He obviously knew it was coming. I told only a few other people. I did not parade it too big since I really did not know how it would all come about. I did not want to make a show out of my giving. Yet, I wanted people to know ahead of time that God was going to perform a miracle.

I started to resolve who the money would go to. I was not going to give it back to the church where it originated. That would be a bit pointless. I committed to the Lord who I would give the money to as soon as the check was cashed.

The morning after Christmas, I made a telephone call to a man who said he wanted to support our ministry. I left a message on his answering machine that said, "(his name); this is David Carmichael. A while back you told me you wanted to support our ministry. I need $15,000.00 for a new vehicle." I told a quick message that invited him to get in on what God was doing. Then I went to the church to see if they would cash their check. There was a problem though. There was only one signature on the check and it required two. I telephoned the man who was supposed to sign the check and asked him if I could come to his house to get his signature. Before I left the church, I told the church secretary the full story. I explained how the Lord had spoken to me to give away $150.00 just prior to getting the check. I told her that it was confirmation that God was now going to give me $1,500.00 to give away as well as a tithe for the $15,000.00 worth of vehicle He was going to provide. Anne had heard similar stories from me before and knew that God had done some marvelous things for us. As usual, she remained pretty even-tempered and just encouraged me on my adventure.

When I went to the gentleman's house (his name is kept confidential so that I might not steal a blessing). I knocked on the door and handed the check to him. He signed it and handed it back to me. Before I left, I told him, "Brother? Do you see these numbers? That decimal place has to move two places to the right." I went on to tell him that my van died and the Lord showed me He was going to provide a vehicle for me. I told him that the $150.00 was a sign that He was beginning to perform a miracle. I did not tell him that I was going to give the money away and I did not tell him about the next prerequisite miracle. When I got into the borrowed VW van to leave, I thanked God for the sign that He was going to fulfill His word to me. Then, God spoke to me again. He told me that somebody I had talked to that morning would give me the $1,500.00 for the vehicle tithe. I had only talked to three people that morning. Anne probably did not have that kind of money. So, that left only two people. In reply, I acknowledged the word from the Lord and thanked Him for it.

As I drove home, I had this deep sense of joy as a result of realizing that I was in the middle of God's miracle. I was overwhelmed that God loved me enough to speak to me and to bless me beyond anything I could ever deserve. Then I thought, "What if that was just my own thought that said someone I talked to today would give me fifteen hundred dollars?" I said to the Lord, "Either way Lord, I will believe you for our need."

I parked the borrowed van in our driveway and walked into the front door. Leslie was just getting off the phone with someone and she had a happy look of urgency on her face. She said, "David; you need to go back to (his name)'s house. He needs to give some money away before the end of the year and he has $1,500.00 that he wants to give you. I broke down, fell to my knees, and cried right there in front of her. I thought I really believed God. When I actually saw Him at work, I could only see myself as a man of unclean lips and an unbelieving heart. I told Leslie what God had told me when I was returning home from the man's house. There was still no way she could comprehend the awe I was in.

When I returned to the man's house, the story got even better. I went inside and told him and his wife everything. I told him that I was going to give the money to someone else. I then told them how God had spoken to me to raise fifteen hundred dollars as a tithe for the vehicle He was going to provide. Then I told them about God telling me to first give away hundred-fifty dollars. I explained how the check entered my previously empty hands just five hours after I heard God speak. Then I told them about God speaking to me just before I drove away from their house earlier. I believed it was important for them to know that they were part of God's miracle. That is when they told me the rest of the story.

The Mrs. had gotten a word from the Lord earlier in the month that they needed to give us some money. She told her husband and he was very skeptical. He said he would do it if the Lord told him as well. My statement about the need, and the $150 being the beginning of a miracle, confirmed to him that his wife had actually heard from the Lord. I would love to know when God actually told her that they needed to give us money. Was it on that Saturday a week before Christmas when Leslie and I were wallowing in our faith versus flesh conflagration? When did the thought come to him to give us $1,500.00? Was it the same moment God told me that someone I talked to that day would give me that amount? We may not ever be clued in to the minute details, but we do know for certain that God was at work.

The day after receiving the check for fifteen hundred dollars, I did the administration necessary to give the money away. I put the check and the paperwork in the mail with a feeling I would have if I were putting gold coins in my piggy bank. Two hours later, I received a telephone call. It was (nameless - for blessings sake) who said he had $1,500.00 that he wanted to give me. He said He had been praying at church on Sunday. The Lord had shown him he needed to give a **first-fruit offering** for money he would receive in January. He intended to give a certain amount of money as well to someone whom he knew had a need. Recently though, the people he was considering giving the money to had found a way to meet their need. He prayed to the Lord asking, "Who should I give the money to." He said that God told him to give the money to us.

Talk about being excited! I told the giver the whole story up to date. Two hours after I gave the fifteen hundred dollars away, It was returned to me. God was performing his miracle and he was doing it in a very neat way.

Episode Fifteen

Presuming Upon God
Part II

Whenever God is at work, I am humbled. Whenever I am at work, I am humiliated. A work of mine normally puffs me up. A work of God, on the other hand, is always bigger than anything I can aspire to.

So far, the story about God's having met our vehicle need seems pretty perfect and fairy-tale like. Notice that I had done nothing to scheme my way into getting money. All of this had been the work of the Lord. He told me to give a first-fruit offering for the vehicle that He was going to provide. He told me to give a first-fruit offering for the first-fruit offering. Then, the Lord started giving me money with which to do His bidding. He also told me, someone that I had talked to that morning would give me $1,500.00. The only thing we had done was to come to the point where we were going to believe God for our need. Sure enough, this whole thing was growing to be a major "signs and wonders" event.

During this time that God was obviously at work, my spiritual eyes were in the trust mode. However, my flesh eyes were presuming that God was going to give me a customized van. We needed a van that could adequately and comfortably carry my family of six. We also needed something that would be able to haul a minimum of eight computers at a time. I knew that God did not tell me that He was going to give me the green customized van that I saw at the dealership. I could not think of a good reason why it should not be the green van. After all, God was the one who stirred our hearts to believe Him for our salvation in this matter. God was the one who told me to give an offering for His answer up front. God was the one who told me to give an offering for the offering. Also, God was the one who was telling other people to give me money in increments of $1,500.00. Fortunately, the only action I could take in the matter was to give away the amount of money that God had designated. I could not go out and buy the green van until I had the total amount in my hand. The Lord also gave me understanding that He was going to meet our need for the van by the end of the year. He did not speak it in so many words; He gave me understanding in my spirit. I knew I had to get rid of both our non-functional vehicles before the end of the year as a step of faith. I sold them each for a dollar to different people who wanted them.

On Thursday of that week, someone called me up and asked me if I needed money for a vehicle. I did not answer them right away. Instead, I told him to tell me the story about why he asked. I told him that God was doing a miracle and I sensed his story would probably be a good one. He had received a new van as a gift the previous summer. He wanted to find a way to tithe what he received. He could see that our passenger van was in really bad shape. He felt prompted by the Lord to help us and he considered giving us his old customized van. Then he realized that it would not really meet our needs because his van was also suffering the consequences of age. So, he sold the van and then just continued to ponder our situation in his spirit. When he heard that our van had given out, he called me to tell me he wanted to give us the tithe for his new van. He wanted to give us $3,000.00 (that's 1,500 x 2). Wow! I then told him the whole story starting from the incident at Sam's club. Signs and wonders were continuing. On Friday, I received another telephone call. It was somebody who had been sacrificially giving to keep us sustained over the previous years. She said she wanted to give us $3,000.00 ($1,500.00 x 2).

Well, the year was nearly over and I thought that God had not given us all the money required to buy the van that we needed. I wrongfully presumed that God would give me the first thing I laid my eyes on. What I can see in retrospect should have been very obvious had I not gotten caught up in idolatry. We needed two vehicles. With the vehicle I had set my eyes on, I could not use it for ministry without stranding my family. Hauling the equipment would also end up trashing the family vehicle.

God had fulfilled His prompting on my spirit. He gave us all the money we needed, and I did not know it. I was confused. The green customized van would not remain unsold for long. I telephoned the dealership on January second and told them I was making progress raising the money. They said I better hurry. It was being detailed so it could be sold at an auction the next weekend. The owner intended to get more than $15,000.00 for it. We only had half the money! So, what should I do? What do most ministry organizations do when they need money?

We carried out our ministry for three years without adequate committed financial support. Often, I received direction from our Elder, Bro. Leonard Riley, that I needed to raise support like other missionaries. However, I found that I could not effectively run a fund raising campaign and fulfill my ministry obligations at the same time. Because I am a man under authority, I tried to raise financial support whenever I could. I was frustrated by it every time. When I put my ministry on hold to raise support, the regular offerings would decrease suddenly and dramatically. When I went back to concentrating all my effort on ministry, we would get abundant unsolicited support. This cycle happened every time I made a concerted effort to raise support rather than doing what God told me to do. I got the impression that God wanted me to trust the Father like His Son showed us. I was supposed to do things as He did them. Do the ministry and let the Father provide. So contrary to modern American missions ministry convention, I just carried out the ministry without the pledge of minimum support. Every now and then, I was tempted again to try to muster up support by directly asking for it in a mailing campaign. My efforts inevitably fell flat, discouraged me, shamed me, and reminded me that God's way is the right way.

Episode Fifteen

Over this van situation, I attempted to interfere with God's miracle using my flesh. I sent out a big hype newsletter trying to muster up $7,500.00 in two weeks. I showed a picture of the nice van that I could buy for a really good deal. As if I was priming a pump, I told about the $7,500.00 that had already come in.

Again, I knew that God had not told me that the van would be ours. Of course, if the money came in, that green custom van is what we would buy. Internally, I was grieving. What kind of miracle is it if I raise the money through hype rather than by the hand of God? Of course, God would get the credit if I actually raised the money, but I knew the confession would not be pure.

The letters went out and I received some money. Just enough to pay for the ink, paper and stamps I had used to send the letters. The van was sold to someone else for $16,500.00. So far, no good! I was failing miserably in the management of God's miracle. What a fool! What an embezzle! What an ultra-maroon! What a connoisseur of fine crow! I had good reason to be humiliated. With my newsletter, I had expanded the number of those who could see the shame of my miscue. I did not report that God told me to buy the van. However, my readers have come to expect me to report works of God rather than works of David. They could see that I had stuck my presumptive neck out with a façade of spirituality.

One day that January, we went back to the music store to check the price of a complete drum set for Jesse. On the way back, we drove past the dealership in shame and pulled up to a Seven-Eleven food store. I went in to buy a classified advertisement magazine, under the guise of looking for used drum sets. I actually wanted to scope-out the price of refrigerators. I was in the process of taking care of the refrigerator miracle by myself. I planned to buy several used refrigerators at auction, and sell them to raise money for one like Leslie described. I wanted to see the going price of used refrigerators so I would know how much money to risk at an auction. I was going to do the work and take care of the need. Of course, God would get the credit. Again, I knew that I was trying to solve my problem, my way, rather than God's way. But again, God was faithful even when I was faithless.

The next day, I scanned through the magazine, with no intention of buying anything. I only wanted to get a sense of the going refrigerator prices. Then one advertisement caught my eye. It was a two-year-old, large-capacity, side-by-side, almond-colored refrigerator with an ice and water dispenser in the door, and glass shelves, for $200.00. I was shocked! Was it true? I read it again. I rushed to the telephone and dialed the number. A lady answered and I asked her if the refrigerator was still for sale? She said I had been the first caller. I asked her if it was functioning properly. She said it ran great and looked great but it was freezing the lettuce she was keeping in the bottom compartment. I told her I would be right over to purchase the unit. I ran to my office and grabbed some money sitting with a bill that was due in the next couple of days. I said a quick flare prayer asking God for the $200.00 that was now needed for the bill lying on my desk. I called my friend Cris Schuzsler and asked him to drive me, along with his trailer, over to pick up this incredibly good deal.

When we got to the seller's house, I asked the lady why she was selling the refrigerator for such a low price. She complained to Frigidaire about the lettuce freezing, and they never sent anyone to fix the problem. One day, nine months after the fact, they stumbled across her complaint. They contacted her and found out she was extremely dissatisfied. Instead of trying to fix the problem, they gave her all her money back and told her she could keep the refrigerator. She bought a new refrigerator and was selling the old one for the difference in the price. Wow! Was I thankful? Yes! Did I think God was blessing me? Yes! The deal was so good, it had to be from God. I was most grateful, and very aware of the fact, that I was relieved of my temptation to resort to my own salvation scheme.

We delivered the refrigerator to my house and had to take its doors off to get it into the house (large capacity). My wife was thrilled and amazed. Since it was two years old, it was actually almond colored instead of the newer cream color. Leslie was overjoyed, she was thankful, and she was praising God. She asked me where I got the money. I told her that I had depleted the money owed for a particular bill. She said that the Lord provided the refrigerator and He would also provide the $200.00 to pay the other bill.

- But wait! There's more!

I got the refrigerator installed just in time to get to church. During the service, Brother Leonard asked me what I was moving into my house when he passed by on his way to church. This was such good news. I stood up and told everybody the story going all the way back to the Sam's Club parking lot incident. I told them about the declaration my wife made about the details of the refrigerator she needed. I told them about my internal struggle to save myself with my buying and selling scheme. I described the refrigerator in detail and then I said I bought it for $200.00. A gasp went out from everybody in the room who knew anything about how much a large refrigerator costs. They all joined me in praising God.

Episode Fifteen

Brother Leonard let the commotion settle down. Then he said, "Let me tell you something. There's more to that story." He was talking as if he had first-hand inside knowledge my refrigerator faith dilemma. He then went on to tell us a part of the story that I did not know. His family member had bought a new refrigerator and had become arbitrarily dissatisfied with it. So, they purchased a new one. Brother Leonard was very aware that our refrigerator desperately needed replacing. So he asked his family member what they were going to do with the old refrigerator. She was going to give it away. He told her that he knew somebody who needed one. Apologizing, she had just promised it to a neighbor of hers. He was disappointed that he had not known about the opportunity sooner. A few days later, he got a letter from his family member. She apologized again for so impulsively giving her refrigerator away to someone who did not really need it. She sent Brother Leonard a check for $200.00, 'to help the family who needed a refrigerator.' A gasp went through the congregation again. He had been holding the $200.00 for nine months asking the Lord what he was supposed to do with it. The Lord just impressed him to hold on to it for the right time.

I knew before that God had brought about the circumstance that got the refrigerator to me for such a deal. Now everybody was in on the miracle. When the realization of the miracle hit me, I started crying profusely. Moments before, I was glib telling everybody about the good van deal that I could give God the credit for. Now, I was sober, and understood again, "Woe is me, for I am a man of unclean lips." God was at work. I was humbled.

This incident made me even more repentant over my presumption regarding the van. I stopped asking for the money, and I tried to just rest in God's promise. Though I had no vehicle, I was assured God was at work by the signs and wonders. Though I still needed a van, I wanted to make sure that I no longer stepped out beyond what God was actually doing.

God did not tell me to write the big fund raising letter when He was providing the money for the van. He did speak to me during the last week of the year 2000. God told me to speak to five specific people. He did not tell me that any of them would give me any money. I knew for sure that God told me to talk to them, but I understood that it might be for their benefit and not mine. At least I went into those conversations with humility rather than presuming upon the Lord.

One of the five people was the man that I left a message on his answering machine asking for $15,000.00. God did not tell me I would get the money but He also did not tell me what to say. So, being that all I could talk to was an answering machine, I just got right to the point. Later, he returned my call. I was able to tell him the story of my situation. Another of the five people was a man at my church, John Stein. Again, God did not tell me why I was supposed to talk to John. I telephoned John and told him just that. Then I told him the whole story beginning with the incident at Sam's Club. He said, "Dave. The first thing that comes to my mind is that you need to go to the auction in Chesapeake." He expounded on his thoughts and said that it seemed to him more than just good sense. He concluded that if God had me call him to hear his advice, it was so that he could say, "Go to the auction." He was praying while he was talking to me and felt that advice was exactly what the Lord wanted him to say.

Well, when God tells me to talk to a particular person about my situation, I better listen. When God told me to talk to those five people, I wrote their names on a post-it notepad. One day I found the notepad and I scratched off the names of the people I had spoken to. Karen Harwood's name remained. She was a friend of mine from my days growing up in California. I struggled with the Lord as to why I should telephone her. It was going to be a little embarrassing. What was I supposed to do? Ask her for money? I knew I was supposed to telephone her right then but I was disobedient. As an excuse, I told the Lord that she would not be home at that time of the day. I sensed that I was in sin but I shrugged the feeling off. I put the note in my pocket and went out for the day to take care of some administration.

I ran into a dear friend, Laverne Johnson, while at the post office. I was thrilled to see her and I told her my story going back to Sam's Club. I told her the good parts where I was really being obedient and where God was working. I also told Laverne where I had really blown it. We laughed. We cried. Laverne pulled a letter out of her post office box while she affirmed me with the things she had learned about trusting God. Looking at the letter wryly, she interrupted herself and asked; "Why am I getting a letter from Gallaudet?"

I knew why she was getting a letter from Gallaudet. It was my fault. The only reason I had even heard of the school is because Karen Harwood graduated from it. The glory of God was revealed again. I was humbled. I pulled the post-it note out of my pocket and showed Karen's name to Laverne. I told her about my struggle with the Lord that morning arguing over whether I should call Karen. I explained how I had been disobedient.

I went home to telephone Karen, expecting to get an answering machine because it was the time that she would be at work. Karen answered the phone. She had taken the day off. I told her the story from the Sam's Club incident to the post office incident. I told her I did not know why God told me to telephone her.

The "no-brainer" benefit of hearing the story is that it encourages each of us to believe that God will intervene in our situations. It is also important to know that the Holy Spirit does speak to us directly. God did not just spin up the Earth to let things fall where they may. God's providence is not like a giant plinko game. He intervenes for His pleasure to show Himself strong on behalf of those who's hearts are loyal to Him.[45]

Even though many people have seen God intervene to deliver us by His mighty hand, they often ask, "What are you doing to solve (the problem)?" There is a constant barrage of 'reason' thrown at me. Since scripture admonishes me to heed sound counsel, I try to make a good showing that I am being responsible. I do things that make sense, sometimes for the sake of my observer's peace of mind. By my own idea, I contacted a wealthy Christian businessman who owned many car dealerships. After I told him our situation, He told me to talk to the President of the company. The President asked me

---

[45] *II Chronicles 16:9*

what I needed. I told him I needed either a full size van or a minivan. If I got a minivan, I would need at least a small pick-up truck to haul my training equipment. By company policy, he could not give cars away. Because of our ministry status, they were willing to sell us a vehicle at their cost. Wow! That was a good deal.

God had given us all the money He was going to give. But in the meantime, someone donated a small pick-up truck. That was wonderful. I had a way to get around town and a way to haul my eight computers to the various training sites. Since I had a means to haul my equipment, a mini-van was a suitable people mover. We looked into mini-vans. We needed something that was relatively new so we would not be distracted by breakdowns. The best price we could get at the dealership, at their cost, was a 1997 Ford Windstar for $9,200.00. The same vehicle was otherwise selling for around $12,000.00. Even for the good deal, we still did not have enough money. I realized the dealership thing was my idea.

Since God told me to talk to John Stein, and John told me to go to the auto auction, that is where I went. I did my homework first. I screened the auction on the Internet. I found out the mileage on each car, if the title was clear, and if the car had a history of damage. I highlighted the ones on my list that showed promise and I went to the auction. I went a few times to inspect cars and get a feel for the proceedings. A decent minivan, that had under a hundred thousand miles on it, was normally sold for well over the amount we had.

One day, I inspected the auction list and found two minivans. One was a good-looking, red, 1998 Ford Windstar with $65,000.00 miles on it. It no doubt would go for about nine thousand or more dollars. The other was a 1997 Chrysler with just under a hundred thousand miles on it. Leslie came in to my office while I was checking out the picture of the vehicles. She saw the red one and started to drool but she realized that it would most likely sell beyond our price range.

I went to the auction alone on that dismally cold day. The air was thick with heavy drizzle. The weather had its effect on the number of people at the auction. I looked at the two mini-vans. The red 1998 was in great shape with minor wear and tear. The front bumper was scuffed and some diffusers were missing in the overhead air-conditioning vents but it otherwise looked good. It was number two on the list of cars going through aisle 'A'. The Chrysler was in really good shape despite its age. It would sell near the end of the auction. Hopefully, other potential buyers would be out of money by the time the Chrysler came around. I had a relatively good chance of getting it for the amount of money I had. I had to spend some money on the truck. I bought tires and support shocks, so it could handle the load I was going to put on it and pass a safety inspection as well. Accounting for sales tax, title fees and the auction fee, I calculated that I could bid up to $6,700.00.

During my previous visits, the auction started at aisle 'A'. The nicer cars that have been repossessed by the bank get first billing on the auction list. The total number of cars gets divided three ways for Aisles 'A', 'B', and 'C'. On that day, they started the sale on aisle 'C'. Nearly everybody rushed to get in on the auction. I could see that the Chrysler was not yet in the line, so I went to aisle 'A' to wait for the 1998 Ford. After a few cars were sold on Aisle 'C', the other auctioneers showed up for aisles 'A' and 'B'. At aisle 'A', there were five dealers and myself. They were engaging in small-talk with one another and began to take notice of me. On aisle 'C' there were anywhere from seventy five to a hundred people. The aisle 'B' auctioneer called the first car into the stall and started his auction. About thirty people turned away from the excitement in aisle 'C' and got in on the aisle 'B' action. Just then, the first car rolled into aisle 'A'. It sold in a flash at a low wholesale price to one of the five gentlemen with a white customer sticker (dealer) on his shirt. Some of the people in aisle 'B' noticed that aisle 'A' had opened up. By the time car number two, the red 1998 Windstar, showed up. Three other people with a yellow customer sticker, like mine, came over to my aisle.

I have been to many auctions. I find that the auctioneers will immediately raise the bid in increments by how many people raise their hands at the opening bid. I don't bid until I hear, "Going once." I stand in the back of the crowd close enough for the auctioneer to readily see me. There, I can see all the other bidders, yet it is difficult for them to watch me. The dealers, and one man with a yellow sticker, all got into the bidding. We who have the yellow stickers on are normally not purchasing a vehicle for resale. So, we normally will out-bid the dealers who have to make a profit.

The bidding rose rapidly starting at $5,000.00. It passed $6,000.00 and my hopes began to diminish. Abruptly, the dealers bidding came to a halt. The bidding was much like choosing who goes first in a street baseball game. $6,000.00 seemed to be the magic dealer threshold at the top of the bat. The man with the yellow sticker's hand happened to be the one that landed. I heard going once before I expected it. I raised my hand subtly but high enough for the auctioneer, who is anxiously looking for bidders. He pointed in my general direction after a very quick glance and pointed right back to the other bidder. The auctioneer glared at him like a hungry wolf looks for a chance to snag a stag, and said, "Sixty-two, sixty-two…." Yellow Sticker readily raised his hand, auctioneer gave a split second glance to me without moving his pointer away from the other man as he said "Sixty-three". I nodded almost imperceptibly. Auctioneer returned his glare to Yellow Sticker prodding him with, "Sixty-four, sixty-four, sixty-four..."

Yellow Sticker hesitated. He looked around the room to see who he was bidding against. By this time there were about fifteen spectators around me and he could not tell that I was his opponent. He turned back to the auctioneer and nodded his head. Auctioneer gave a rapid glance to me with the word "Sixty-five", I nodded subtly, and he pounced right back on Yellow Sticker. The auctioneer treated me as he would a veteran and looked to Yellow Sticker as his victim. He perceived I knew what I wanted and knew how to get it. He knew he could drive the price up by pressuring Yellow Sticker to bid possibly beyond his means. He had prodded Yellow Sticker to go that far, but he would not go to "Sixty-six." I wished that the auctioneer would just reward me with a win for my suave technique. Mr. auctioneer had no twinge of camaraderie however. He

Episode Fifteen

harangued his patsy with "Sixty-five-fifty." Yellow Sticker gave a
"why not?" look and Auctioneer checked me again with "Sixty-six". I
was groaning inside but I returned the usual poker-faced nod and
auctioneer prodded Yellow Sticker again, "Sixty-seven, Sixty-
seven,…." Yellow sticker was obviously struggling with whether he
could afford a win. Auctioneer adjusted to Yellow Sticker's
hesitation by reducing the offer to "Sixty-six-fifty, Sixty-six-fifty,..."
Yellow sticker weighed in again and the auctioneer flashed my limit at
me, "Sixty-seven". I nodded in the rhythm we had established.

Yellow sticker had figured out who was bidding against him by
this time. Most likely, by now, everyone there figured that he was
being tempted beyond his means. He looked straight at me and sized
me up. All I gave him was the stoic look I had copied from the
dealers. Inside and outside I was sweating. I was on a precipice and
so was he. We both knew it about him but he did not know it about
me. He hesitated; talked to his wife he looked back at the auctioneer
who was now sending him "Sixty-seven-fifty" expressed as a
question. Auctioneer threatened Yellow Sticker with the rise of his
gavel. I was groaning. Yellow Sticker gave a slight rise to his
countenance and then????? Waved the dealer off. "Sold for sixty-
seven hundred dollars."

The adrenaline from the conflict had numbed my brain and given me tunnel vision. It took a while for me to realize what happened. I had won the bid. All the money had been spent. God had provided a truck and now we owned a really nice mini-van free and clear. Wow!

What did I learn in all of this? "Wait and see!" That phrase, "Wait and see!", needs to be my motto in every situation that I know is instigated by God. When I see the glory of God showing up, it is best for me to keep my mouth shut, my head low, and my eyes shielded. Those blessings that are literally a miraculous work from God's mighty hand are just as fearful as His judgement. It reminds me of a scripture that is related to our spiritual salvation. Yet, I see now that it cannot be separated from His salvation in all things. "Not by works of righteousness which we have done, but according to His mercy He saved us,...."[46]

---

[46] *Titus 3:5*

Episode Sixteen

Train Your Relief

I mentioned in the previous chapter that I was the Worship Pastor at Restoration Church in Hampton, Virginia. That came about when our Senior Pastor called me, literally on the phone, in April of 2000. He was contemplating what he would do to find someone for the position. He was not looking forward to the long term search for someone with the proper qualifications. Then, the Lord prompted him with my name. After continuing his discussion in prayer with the Lord, he concluded that he was supposed to invite me to come serve.

When I was called, I knew in my spirit that it was the right thing at the right time. Though I did not read music, except at an elementary level, God had prepared me for the music ministry. The words and visions God had given to Leslie and me, to Renee' Riley, and to Cindy Everett were indelibly etched in my mind. I knew God intended to do a good work using me, and eventually Leslie, in a music ministry.

Coincidentally, the paid position came at a very critical time. I had some personal bills, relating to things other than ministry, that were starting to come due in earnest. It was important for me to keep those costs separate from the support I was getting through Educational Christian Ministries. The monthly pay from the music position would take care of those particular personal bills that were growing monthly.

The Worship Pastor position was a marvelous, yet grave, responsibility. I was challenged beyond my musical training. More importantly, I realized how desperately I needed to be prayed up. The worship service is not really about music. It is about the will of the Lord being revealed and carried out. It was critical for me to hear what God intended to do each week, and plan the music correspondingly.

Very consistently, God revealed Himself and His plans to me as I prepared for the worship services. The music format gave way to the prophetic message. Sometimes, a Praise Team member would be tempted to scoff at my selections of music. There was no way for me to fully communicate the sense I had that God was moving in a particular way. They had no way of knowing whether my strange choices were from divine inspiration or because I was musically unsophisticated. Yet, for the most part, God glorified Himself. There were a great many times when the sermon and the music seemed to have been deliberately coordinated.

After a little over a year as Worship Pastor, I was told that I was to attend a retreat with the Elders and other Pastors. We were going to spend time praying and having serious discussions about the Lord's vision for our church. I had many personal opinions about what ought to be part of the church vision. I knew, however, that my opinions were not what the church needed. The church needed a vision from God. Therefore, I began to pray earnestly. I asked God to show me what I needed to take to the meeting as my understanding of what He intended for our church's future.

All of the sudden, that now familiar prompting of the Holy Spirit hit me strongly. God revealed to me that He intended that I be out of the Worship Pastor position by the end of May 2003. I was shocked. I checked again in prayer if that was right. I was assured to the depth of my spirit that God's plan was that I complete my task as Worship Pastor by that time. So, I believed it, received it, and determined in my heart to act on it. I told the Lord, "okay Lord, I will tell them that my ministry as Worship Pastor will conclude May 2003." I then asked God what I would be doing after that time. He would not tell me. I asked Him how I would be able to pay those demanding personal debts [47]. He gave me no answer. Trusting Him was the obvious implication.

Here was a situation where God revealed only part of his will and only part of his plan. Like the mobile home incident, I was not to know the details of the outcome, only the part that required my obedience. God's prompting about the demise of my part-time ministry position caused me to pray diligently as the day of our retreat approached. I had a reverent confidence about my future as I entered our time of retreat.

I had some anxiety going into the meeting. During my short tenure as Worship Pastor, I introduced some controversy relating to the daily administration of the church ministry. I was not sure whether some of the elders trusted me. Some of my stances of faith made me appear as somewhat of a maverick. I intended to be extremely careful with

---

[47] *Accumulated by Legal bills from a challenge to the Navy's actions mentioned in Episode Eight.*

my words and to put on my best air of maturity and stability.

We opened with prayer. My mask of reasonableness did not stay on for long. After there were a few opening words about what we came to discuss, I interjected. 'Gentlemen! Before we begin, I need to tell you what God told me as I was in prayer, preparing for this meeting. I knew I did not want to bring my own opinions to the table. I wanted God to give me His vision. Suddenly, the Lord interrupted my prayer and told me I was supposed to conclude my ministry as Worship Pastor by May of 2003.' As I sort of expected, they took offence, at first. It was the reaction of their flesh that soon became buffered by the spirit. They knew that they had to consider that I had actually heard from God. The Senior Pastor, with a bit of an agitated look on his face said, "What are you going to do then? What are you scheming?" He did not mean it as an insult. He presumed that I might have some preoccupation that had a time-line. "Nothing. I don't have any schemes, except for unemployment. The Lord didn't show me what He wanted me to do afterward, only that He wanted me out of the job."

I did not know before the meeting what would be brought up by the Senior Pastor, but the Lord did. When we got to the portion of the outline concerning the worship ministry, our pastor voiced his vision. He ordered a much expanded music ministry that would include a choir and an orchestra. What he described required a full-time minister who was both trained and called for such a ministry. I can't even read music beyond the "first grade" level. Initially, I was terrified of the thought of such a huge responsibility. Then I was quite relieved thinking that I would be out of the job and the task would be left to somebody else.

I then asked if there was a time-line. "A choir in one-year and an orchestra in two years" was the response. My relieved expectation of not having to shoulder the task was shattered. I did an immediate flare prayer. My flesh was writhing. How would I appease the Praise Team who would feel displaced? How would I have the time to do the Senior Pastor's tasking and still be able to fulfill my main ministry duties? How would I do that which I am not trained to do?

My knee-jerk thought came from a phrase I often heard while in the military, "Not on my watch! Not in my Navy!" I realized right-away that I needed to put my flesh back in its box. I was a man under authority. If that is what the leadership asked for, that is what the leadership gets. I did voice my concerns, doubts and reservations about the feasibility of the mandate. I explained the magnitude of what it would take to do it right. I told them that they described the duties

269

of someone in a full-time position, who was fully trained. With each statement, the mandate was reinforced. So, I told them that I was a man under authority. I would do what I was given to do.

I explained to the Elders and other Pastors that it was obvious to me why God told me to be conclude my position there by May 2003. They needed someone much more equipped than I was. I told them I would prepare the worship ministry for my relief. I promised to organize a choir and expand the band. That way, there would be structure already in place so my relief would not have to start from scratch.

Not long after the word God gave me in 1992 to prepare myself for music, I obtained a digital piano as a gift from my mother. I began to read and learn the Prodigal Son Suite by the late Keith Green. I began to learn to play it closely enough to resemble the original so that the untrained ear could not tell the difference. Leslie would sing the song as I played it. I cannot play and sing the song at the same time without getting too emotional to sing. God used the song to minister to me deep into my soul. Les and I would discuss ways that the song might be used to minister to others in a church service. We concluded that the song ought to be done to a full-blown drama. Each verse of the song should be a segue into the next scene.

Over the years the concept solidified in our hearts and minds. Periodically, when my wife and I would go out on a date to spend time together, she would say let's talk about "The Prodigal". We mulled it over again sometimes in mild argument, but ultimately concluding with agreement on how it should be done. It began to Dawn on me, not long after our vision retreat, that The Prodigal might be used as the perfect medium to initiate a choir and orchestra. It would also serve as a catalyst for a broader worship ministry at Restoration Church. I spent a few months in prayer over it. I really sensed that the Holy Spirit confirmed in my heart that it was the right course to take.

I began to count the cost. It would take at least six months to carry it out. I needed several months before-hand to write the script; and to find, prepare and arrange music suitable to my vision. I needed music to enable the choir to effectively complement the message and mood of the musical drama. Physically, mentally an emotionally, I was drained at the outset. But spiritually, I became zealous each time I had to open my mouth to speak the vision.

After Christmas of 2001 the Praise Team began to ask about the special music I planned for Resurrection Sunday. They knew we needed to get to work by January to actually make it come off "special". I had bad news and good news. The bad news was, the resurrection celebration would be rather ordinary. We would do music, that we knew well, that was keeping with the theme of the day. We had a bigger project planned for the end of the summer or early fall.

Then I began to prophesy. It was not just wishful thinking, it was an utterance of faith. As I began to speak, I felt the presence of Lord. I described each scene as it would be played out. I described the movements of music and how they would convey the mood of the story segments. The Praise Team easily imagined the magnitude of the production. The number of singers, musicians, actors, costumes, staging and other logistics that the production required was daunting. They were put back by the whole scheme. For the most part, they did not want to have anything to do with it.

When casting a vision, it is extremely important to speak the vision, or project, and how it is going to be accomplished. Habukuk 2:2 says, "Write the vision, and make it plain upon tablets, that he may run that reads it." In the physical realm, you describe a plan in depth in order to have experienced-others verify that the plan is at least feasible. In the physical realm, all your plans must prove possible with a means you have available to accomplish them. With a spiritually conceived plan however, your plans are not required to be possible by any physical means.

Such a vision, that appears physically impossible, may be a huge stumbling block to those who cannot perceive it with eyes of faith. If people do not see that a project is possible "physically", they most likely will not be willing to lend their name to it. They might offer some time as token support. However, they will not associate themselves with your project to the point of sharing your potential humiliation or some other tangible loss.

Does God only give some small vision that we are able to accomplish without his help or intervention?

I confided the vision so precisely to the Praise Team, many of them thought it was prepackaged with script and music already prepared. Even then, they believed that it was too big for us to do. One brother said to me, "You don't think of trying something small to start with, do you?" Rather than trying to convince him of its reasonableness, I replied, "I can't help it. God did not give me anything small, only this." They also did not believe that I could muster the participation or resources needed to pull it off. I had to consider that they might be right as far as getting people to participate. As far as 'pulling it off', I had no choice. 'Pull it off' is what I had to do. I published the vision and began to solicit participation.

The initial response was very small. I was not daunted however because I knew the Lord's pleasure was in it. We would carry out the production even if we had people playing multiple parts; had a choir of only a few singers, and had the music played by a computer. It was most important to find people of faith who wanted to get in on what the Lord was doing. It was a Gideon moment.

The first thing I did was to boldly confess the whole vision whenever I could. It either repulsed people or inspired them. I made no effort to recruit those people who it repulsed. Those who only seemed confused or doubtful, I encouraged them to join us. At the same time, I confounded them with more grandiose details. I discouraged their eyes of flesh and instilled just a little bit of natural fear in their hearts. I then reminded them that "with God, all things are possible." We were going to overcome motivated by faith, not fear.

One of the more interesting characters in all of this was my Senior Pastor. He is a man who demonstrates the definition of love when considering the passage, "By this all men shall know that you are my disciples. If you have love for one another." He is also a stickler for order, neatness and planning. In his heart he no doubt wanted to see it all come to pass. From the beginning of the project however, I had no way of keeping him in his comfort zone. Brother Leonard was rightfully concerned that whatever we did, we did well. Naturally, he had questions that started with the words "How are you going to...?" My seemingly irresponsible response in most cases was, "I don't know." As well, one of my musicians, asked, "Where did you get the music arrangements?" My response, "I've not arranged the music yet." When I did answer the "how you gonna" questions, the answer usually led to bigger "how you gonna" questions. Fortunately, twenty years before, Brother Leonard had mentored a young man who also had big visions that somehow came to pass as they simultaneously united the body in ministry. Thus, Brother Leonard's love readily overrode any temptation to consternation he might have had over the whole thing. He became my biggest promoter.

Two days before the curtain time, Brother Leonard asked if we were going to have a curtain. I said "Yes". "Where is it?" My response, "We've not made it yet." Good grief-rolled across his silent face. Sternly he said, "Well! You better get working on it." "We are!" The morning of curtain call, Brother Leonard asked again, "Have you got a curtain?" Me: "Yes, but no curtain rail." Brother Leonard: "What are you going to do without a curtain?" Me: "We're going to have a curtain."

Episode Sixteen

Minutes before curtain call, the curtain and rail were mounted but not working properly. With a whole lot of oil and a few modifications, it was functional two minutes before show-time.

I was told that I did a beautiful job of delegating. I had to confess a correction. I delegated very little. Really, I dropped the ball in every critical area. In each case, the Lord raised someone to pick up the ball and run with it. Each participant did not pick up a well-ordered task and provide the service. They shouldered the responsibility to manufacture a product suited to the vision.

I intended to direct the play, cast the parts and coach the actors. I was then going to assign an assistant director. They would oversee the production while I turned to my acting role. Before I could do that, I had to get the orchestra familiar with music that had not yet been arranged. It took me hundreds of hours to arrange music using a computer program. I would finish a small portion at a time, and then get our budding orchestra to work through it. Thus, I was taken out of the overseer role, and pigeon-holed as the preliminary orchestra director. Meanwhile, Hank (otherwise known as Kenny D'Auria) was supposed to lead the choir. He ended up casting, coaching, and blocking all the scenes in my absence. In reality, all the scenes were cast, final-scripted and blocked by the participants with Kenny acting as a facilitator.

While Kenny was busy with the preliminary directing, his wife Delia jump-started the choir. She even provided some needed elementary music reading and vocal training. My lighting director, Tim Wright, morphed into being the overall producer/director. Once the music was arranged and introduced to the orchestra, Michael Carpenter took over as orchestra director. He was the man for the job. He immediately took things I had arranged and threw superfluous notes away. I was not at all offended. I was relieved. Someone who was very gifted, and thorough, made sure the music sounded good. Praise God! I fell in line simply as an actor playing the role of the father. Leslie choreographed some superb dances, she designed the costumes, and she spearheaded the work to make the costumes and mount the couple hundred feet of stage curtains.

The only one whose role remained constant was "Rich Meadows", the sound guy. He turned our acoustically dysfunctional sanctuary into a Hampton version of Carnegie Hall. After a couple showings we found out that the audience thought we were using professionally produced music on a background CD. It was not just because the orchestra was out of view. It was because of the quality of the musical performance, mixing and cueing. One night we had the orchestra play some random notes at the end of the show to prove to the audience that the music was live. People still did not believe it. They thought somebody turned on a CD and just moved around the disk with their hand to make random noise. Finally, at the end of our last performance, we brought them out on stage to prove their existence. Many other people sacrificed resources of time, money and work to make "The Prodigal" a huge success.

Sometimes the Lord speaks clearly in a mandate. Some times He just steers me down a path as I seek His face and His kingdom. The Prodigal vision was like that. It was something that the lord cultivated in our hearts for many years. The Prodigal may have been used by the Lord to convey the gospel to some who came to see it. I believe it is a very useful tool for that purpose. I do not believe that was the reason God gave Leslie and me the vision for it. We do not know all the plans that the Lord had for The Prodigal. What we can see in hindsight is that God spoke the vision. It was extremely timely. It solidified a spirit of faith within our congregation and it has birthed other ministry initiatives. Well over a hundred people in our church participated in the production. It would not have happened if we had limited our plans and actions to those things that are easy to conclude as reasonably sure. The Prodigal reminded us that, like other works of faith, we must seek and recognize the leading of the Holy Spirit, and then obey.

That summer of preparing for the Prodigal, I diligently sought the Lord's face and will concerning our future. I pondered God's directive to turn-over the music ministry. The Lord confirmed to me that it was the right thing to do. Still, God did not show me anything passed May 31, 2003. When I was steeped in prayer, I was in perfect peace and felt the Lord's pleasure in it.

My parallel search for the Lord's will involved my primary ministry. I was perpetually seeking clear direction from the Lord but I was not getting any inspiration. Since the Lord was freeing up a significant amount of my time, He must have some new wave of activity planned for that ministry. However, I did not get any vision regarding the growth or continuance of the computer training evangelism. Instead, God was telling me "Stop! Be still!". At first, I believed that God wanted me to stop worrying about the future after May 2003. The more I prayed about it, the more I came to realize that God literally wanted me to stop. Continuing my activities, including the ministry functions I was performing, would amount to sin.

The thing that is "right to do" on it's face very well may be wicked if it is contrary to God's plan. I understood. God wanted me to stop, and seek His face. I was to take a sabbatical. Any work I did beyond May 31, 2003, without His permission, would, in effect, be sinful. Logically, it made sense as far as a Biblical perspective. It makes sense to put spending time with God as the absolute priority, especially in ministry.

When I was in a state of prayer, I found myself in a state of faith. I understood perfectly that God intended to demonstrate His power in and through our lives but it would only come at the cost of complete submission. When I was not in a state of prayer, I was extremely troubled. How can I justify my financial support when all I am doing (supposedly) is sitting around praying for a year? Being in complete submission also entails complete reliance upon God for our survival. In our case, reliance upon God for our survival generally entails reliance on other people. In my natural mode of thinking, reliance on other people means that I am a "Freeloader." Every part of my being writhes with that thought.

It is sort of shameful that every time God speaks to me, I try to think myself out of obedience. Even Moses demonstrated that natural tendency. He questioned whether it was really God speaking to him. He questioned the validity of his tasking based upon what he believed others would think. He questioned whether he was worthy of God's lofty assignment.

My first question was, "Is that really God speaking?"[48] It is the same question that arises every time He speaks. Every time God speaks to me, His mandate wars against my flesh. I wrongly justify my hesitance to appease my guilt for not readily obeying. I try to convince myself that I am just making sure the word is from the Lord and Biblically sound. It is, in most cases, that I am not really doing the noble thing that I claim to be doing. It is most often that I don't really want to hear what God is saying to me.

The next thought that comes to mind is the fear of humiliation, ridicule, scorn, and gossip that will ensue if I do God's bidding.[49] There have been times that I acted on faith in the past, and it drove some people in church away from me. Those who were alienated thought I had 'gone off the deep end'. In possibly every case, they got their information askew through the grapevine. Ridicule, scorn, and etceteras, will come, but ultimately it is a part of the cost of discipleship.

Finally, like Moses, I doubt God. I doubt His willingness to allow

---

[48] *Exodus 3:13*
[49] *Exodus 4:1*

me to participate because of my "belief" that I am not worth His efforts to use me.[50] Who am I to spend time isolated with the Lord over the next year in order for Him to reveal Himself and His plans for me? Who am I to be used by God for a specific and special purpose? By faith, I know that God wants to use me, to glorify Himself, because I have made myself available; not because I am notable.

In order to facilitate a smooth transition to a new worship leader, we brought Ken D'Auria on as my assistant in January 2003. We began slowly working him into the duties. We worked up a special music program for the Resurrection Celebration weekend as a prelude to a choir and orchestra ministry. We also incorporated "human video" drama as a worship medium. As Hank[51] started shouldering a majority of my duties, I started feeling the pangs of the conclusion of my ministry as Worship Pastor. I also started doing the math in my head about how much money would no longer be available every month. I got twinges of fear. During prayer, I was reminded that God

---

[50] *Exodus 4:10*

[51] *Inside joke! Kenny asked me if I changed people's names in the book to protect their identity. He asked me if I called him "Hank" or something. Thus, his "handle" is "Hank."*

had ordained the cessation of my ministry position. I had to conclude that He would provide for my needs. Yet, by mid-May, the temptation to despair became more intense. I had five certain bills that were paid by the music ministry check. We, again, found ourselves in the obedience mode without the faith to enjoy what we were doing.

It is amazing how your body will react to worry just like it does when it is being presently challenged by danger. Your heart beat speeds up, your breathing becomes rapid and shallow. These things started happening to me as I began to think about the consequences of not having the money needed to pay my monthly requirements. I think one of the reasons that worry about the future is so stressful, is because I am trying to think of a solution that I can accomplish. Fear slips in when I am not getting any reasonable ideas about how to solve my problem. As I think of possible solutions, I become increasingly fearful as the time that I need to accomplish the task begins to slip away.

It is like the time I was on a mission to help my wife make my daughter's fourteenth birthday a real hit. We designed a photograph scavenger hunt that had a lot of crazy things that the kids had to do. One idea was to put a photograph, showing the location of the next clue, on a pier piling jutting out into the Chesapeake Bay. To put the photo where we needed it, I got into an inflatable rubber raft. I took a paddle, some small nails, a hammer, and the laminated photograph. I rowed out to the end of the pier and found that nailing a picture to the pier piling was going to be very difficult. The waves lifted me up and down, and the current pulled me away from the pier. I thought I could hold myself to the pier with my arm wrapped around the piling. Then I would accomplish my task with my free hand. The first, and most critical, difficulty I encountered was barnacles. I sliced a gruesomely deep cut on my thumb when I reached around and pulled myself to the piling. Nevertheless, I adjusted the position of my hand and pulled the raft tightly to the pole. Then reality hit my brain and look of horror adorned my face. If the barnacles slashed my hand so easily, what was it going to do to the raft? With that realization, I was shocked that I had not yet ripped a hole in the raft. I rushed to get the raft away from the piling. Then, of course, the sound of ripping rubber, and the gurgling of air rushing into the water, sent a surge of terror into my soul.

It might not have been so bad had I not been lying on my back in the raft. The raft was flattening firstly at my shoulders, so my neck and shoulders began to submerge. My heart started to race and I started panting and gasping for air. Part of the rush of fear was due to the notion I had that the raft would by gone in a matter of three or four seconds. I thought, oh great! I am going to drown. Then I reminded myself that I was a good swimmer. But how was I going to swim with a hammer, nails, paddle and photograph in my hands? I was afraid to abandon ship for fear that I would lose my precious cargo. Fortunately, the raft was taking a good ten to fifteen seconds to deflate. I realized also that I actually might be able to stand up. By about the ten second point, I gathered everything I had into one hand and I did a back summersault into the water. I intended to either walk ashore, or swim with my one available hand. The water was much deeper than over my head. When I came up for air, I noticed the raft was still partially inflated at its stern. I realized something that also had not occurred to my terror stricken brain. I still had a floatation device available. I tucked the raft in the pit of my arm, and was able to rest a little, while I used the oar to paddle ashore.

This strange pseudo survival tale is here to illustrate where I experienced similar sensations of fear like unto my impending $1,250.00 pay cut. At first, I panicked. Then I started the struggle for survival. Then I realized that my only real threat was fear. When I got back on track with what I had learned over the years, I found that survival took care of itself. As Commodore Cosgriff used to tell us, "In the heat of the battle, stick to the plan!" The preplanned response that God has taught us for these situations is, "Seek ye first the kingdom of God and His righteousness. And all these other things will be added as well."

Episode Seventeen

"What's next?"

I continued to minister as part-time "Worship Pastor" through May of 2003 at Restoration Church - Phoebus Baptist. The church paid me at the beginning of each month prior to my rendering any service. So, on June 1st, I was not going to be paid for the work I did in May. I had a very busy month turning over my part-time ministry. Also, I had a full schedule with my evangelism and job skill training ministry. There was no way, in May, to generate income for the shortfall that would come in June.

On the Morning of May 31st, we were completely out of cash except for a couple of dollars of loose change. In one way, it was very encouraging. Since I was certain that God was leading us into the situation, I knew the lack of cash the day before unemployment was not a sign of doom. Instead, it gave me zeal for what I believed would be an exciting demonstration of God's power. The day started with our church taking its turn to feed the homeless and providing other ministries at Zoe Community Church. As Worship Pastor, I was responsible to provide worship music prior to the meal being served. The leader of our youth praise band agreed to provide the music ministry for that day. That freed me to concentrate on providing the short message between the music and the meal.

It was a good day for me to be required to provide a sermonette. I needed to be seeking God's presence and His word continually. Not only for the message I had to deliver, but for the entire day. I was preparing for what I believed to be a year of divine inspiration and intervention. I really needed to sense the presence of God in order to have the faith to just get through that day.

I had a fairly tough crowd to preach to. They were used to ignoring messages that are being preached at them. Several people were just tolerating the sermon while they waited for the food. A few started being a bit disruptive. God was gracious however.

I preached about the parable of the master hiring laborers for his field. I modified the parable and used a modern situation that they all were familiar with. I described a local corner where day laborers hang out. A man came by looking for workers to move some stuff around in his warehouse. He came by the corner at 6:00 a.m. and found a group of men and women ready to go to work. He invited them to come work the whole day for $60.00. My audience knew that the normal rate they could expect was $50.00. The sixty dollar value made them pick their heads up a bit and take note that the amount promised was more than fair. Since they were all familiar with the scenario, the disruptions started to settle down. The warehouse owner needed more workers. He went back to the corner and found those late sleepers at 9:00 a.m. My audience laughed a bit. When I told them the warehouse owner promised to pay them sixty dollars as well, I had a captive audience.

There was so much stuff to be moved and there were not yet enough workers to get the job done. So, he went back and found a group hanging out on the same corner at noon and he hired them as well. At 3:00 he still needed a few more hands to get the job done so he ventured back to 25th and Jefferson Avenue. He found a group socializing on the corner. He asked them what they had been doing all day and if they had any interest in work. They were all a bit embarrassed that they had spent the whole day carousing. Even so, he asked them to work for him to get all the stuff moved in his warehouse. They agreed but said they needed to be back by 4:30 so they could get a ride to the shelter. The warehouse man promised to get them back on time and he put them to work.

He brought everyone back at 4:30 and began to pay them. I told the audience that the first group got what was promised them. My listeners realized the price was fair but the first ones had not gotten as good a deal as the 9 o'clock crowd. I told them that the noon crowd was paid sixty dollars as well. Several people in the audience grinned and made comments about what a good deal that was. Then I told them that the 3:00 p.m. crowd also got sixty dollars for their short term of labor. Most of the audience was angry with the three o'clock crowd and some laughed because they got away with such a good deal.

I explained to my audience that I got the story from Jesus out of the Bible. I said many of them were like the 3 o'clock crowd. They had spent their whole life wasting time and carousing. They believed that there was no hope for them to ever obtain a reward from God, only judgement. They knew that their time was short and the days of their life would soon be over. They believed that God would not consider them worthy to come work for Him at such a late hour. Then I told them that the late hour did not matter. God had prepared the same reward for them as the reward given to those who submitted to God at the beginning of their life.

I also talked about liberty, the woman at the well, the living water, and being captive or being possessed rather than having possessions. We all began to sense the presence of the Holy Spirit. I began to see several people, who I thought were the toughest cases, begin to tear up and bow their heads. God was working.

We gave an invitation for people to respond to what God was doing in them. There was some follow-on ministry for those who were responding. Eventually, the time of food, music and fellowship was complete and everyone went on with their day.

All my Pre-June-1st tasks were complete. I had fulfilled all the responsibilities of my calling as Worship Pastor at Restoration Church. Also, we were flat broke. I knew there had to be a miracle on the way. There was no other means available to us.

After sunset, someone brought us thirty dollars. The gift was encouraging but it certainly would not sustain us. Leslie and I were still stressed thinking about our financial predicament. We both knew we needed what we call a "staff meeting". We put our oldest child in charge and headed out to look for a quiet place to talk while we ate a snack. We left after 9:30, on a Saturday night. There was no suitable place open that met our preferences of quietness, decent food, and a decent price. French fries and a drink in the McDonald's the parking lot would have to suffice. Once that was decided, we naturally found our conversation going right to the situation at hand.

The primary concern I had was the five credit card bills that came in every month. They had sustained us through our religious liberty battle that was continuing to rage. The five bills totaled over nine hundred dollars every month. The music ministry income took care of that financial need.

Then, we had a catastrophe that I should have expected given the stress of the situation. Leslie started venting. What she said is not what we need to chronicle here. We need to record our struggle between the pangs of self preservation and reliance upon God for our survival. Leslie was again experiencing a natural fear from being subjected to the potential consequences of my actions. Again, I was the one who received direct instruction from the Lord to step out of the Worship Pastor position. Leslie's problem was that she did not hear the voice of the Lord in this matter. I did. All she could see was me pulling the plug on her life-raft just when she was most comfortable in it.

Like the event at Sam's Club. Speaking the truth about God's goodness over the years was the key to keeping our head above the figurative waters. We both had to acknowledge that God had truly spoken before. He had shown Himself strong by His mighty hand in every situation where He called us to trust upon Him. After a heated spiritual debate, that at least came to a positive confession, we went home for some badly needed sleep.

I sought the Lord's face in earnest Sunday morning, June 1st, 2003. I began to pray. I asked God to show me what I needed to do to take care of the credit card bills. How was I supposed to do what was necessary to earn money to pay those bills and still have time sanctified for a Sabbatical? As my spirit groaned in prayer, the Lord began to give me peace. I was assured that my tasking was to seek God's face. He would show me what I was supposed to do. I was His employee. He would also show me what I was allowed to do any time that might be considered my own. I was permitted to put whatever God showed me into book form or teaching lessons for the future. I was inspired to take a portion of writing I had made a couple years before and write a book about faith. It would be a perpetual sermon for others who needed the encouragement. I understood that my time of sabbatical would be very productive. It would be productive for the purpose of God's kingdom.

Again, there are times when God speaks a specific word that requires specific obedience. Then there are times when God gives me understanding. I know the right thing to do, and conversely, the wrong thing to do. I remind myself that what might be considered okay to do from a earthly perspective may be wrong from God's perspective. On Sunday morning, June 1st, 2003, God gave me understanding. The work (livelihood) God wanted me to do was to get close to Him, seek Him, write down what He said, and then do it! I needed to focus my time on seeking and doing His specific will, rather than spending my time trying to save myself. He assured me that I was not supposed to worry about the money needed for the next round of bills due in the next few days. He would take care of it.

After the intensive prayer time, I went downstairs to begin editing the book I started years ago. After I finished editing the first chapter called "A Still Small voice", I found it was time to go to church. I was so excited about what God was doing, I wanted to make a copy of my work to give others to have a first glimpse. Printing out a couple of copies of the portion I edited made me late. I slipped into church during the welcome time and joined my family in our normal seating area. It was important for me to make sure I was at church that day. Many people wondered if I was going to find another church to go to after I stepped down from my position. I could not let myself be conspicuously absent.

The sermon was awesome and right on time. It was about getting, and focusing on, a vision from the Lord. I was excited about all the things the Pastor was saying. Right in the middle of the sermon, my attention to the Pastor was interrupted with a sudden thought. "Faith – The Final Frontier." I thought it was kind of a funny phrase. It had a subtle twinge of Divine inspiration. I wondered to myself why that thought had come to my mind. I had already decided the book was to be called "A Still Small Voice." The Lord confirmed to me that the new title summed up the focus and spirit of the book. I wrote it down on the first page of the sample chapter I had printed that morning. I felt a deep sense of satisfaction that the title was settled. I returned my attention to the message from the pulpit.

At the end of the service, our new Senior Pastor, David Bounds, asked Leslie and me to come forward. Addressing the congregation, he summed up our ministry over the previous three years. He went on to say that God was calling us to move on to other things. He asked "the gentleman to come forward" so they could take up an offering for us as a gift of appreciation. Pastor David knew I was stressed over the fact that I was not going to get a pay check that month. I told him about the five bills that were being paid every month because of my music ministry income. I wondered whether the offering was a work of our combined flesh or a work of the Lord. Our church was many thousands of dollars below budget and recently had special offerings taken for other missionaries. Any offering for us might probably be very meager. But on the other hand, God might very well use it to perform the miracle we needed. I rendered a quick prayer, "Lord? Are you going to use this to take care of those bills?" (no answer) "Well, either way, if it's only a hundred bucks, I'll take the kids camping or something. I will just trust You to do whatever You are going to do." Pastor David prayed for us and then called the men forward to take up the offering.

On Monday, I was called in to the office to sign the check from the offering. It was in the amount of $891.00. I was shocked at the large gift. Still, I had really hoped that God would perform a miracle through it. It did not seem to meet the amount of what was usually required; about $915.00. I believed the offering would have met our total need if it was from the Lord. I was a little disappointed. I was not going to be able to tell people that God met my need completely on my first day of "unemployment".

On Tuesday, I picked up the $891.00 offering in cash from the church. I also picked up the money that the church provides to us as missionaries. I headed to the post office to get the last of those five bills and to purchase money orders to pay them. I traveled to the post office with apprehension. I was in a dilemma about how what to do about the difference in the amount of the bills and the amount of the offering. Though I have a discretionary personal spending allowance, I did not want to set a precedent of using E.C.M. derived money to pay my legal bills. I knew in my heart that using that resource was a flesh solution and not one of faith. However, E.C.M. money was now my only means of survival. I asked the Lord what I should do. Should I not pay one of the five bills when the love offering money fell short? If the Lord told me to pay the bills with my discretionary ECM money, I would do it. If not, I would have to decide which bill to not pay. If the Lord gave me the go-ahead to use ECM derived money, should I pay more than the minimum listed? The Lord answered me very clearly. "Just make the payment asked for on the bill." I presumed that meant it was okay to use whatever money I had.

When I opened each of the envelopes, on first glance, the amounts owed seemed to be less than I had expected. I wrote the amount listed for each minimum payment in the box provided. I normally do not tally up the amount of the bills and I did not see the necessity of doing it now. Mr. Burrell, the postman, would tell me the amount when he tallied up all the postal money orders. I sensed in my spirit that the specific amount was important. I looked at the numbers. I calculated right away that three nines made twenty-seven and four more made thirty-one. Noooo! Could it be? Had the Lord met the amount to the very dollar? I brushed the thought aside as just wishful thinking. I wrote each bill amount on my hand: 399, 189, 179, 110, 14. Then I looked in wonder as I tallied it up. $891.00. I then pulled the cash out of my pocket and counted it again to make sure I was not dreaming. $891.00. Then I counted the amount written on my hand again.

I made this kind of caveman sounding grunt as I was overwhelmed in my standard "woe is me" reaction. I turned to the lady standing next to me who looked at me with concern wondering if I had just become sick. I had to tell her. I turned my left palm toward her so she could see my tally and I said, "This is a miracle." With teary eyes and a wavering voice, I turned to the people in line behind me and told the whole story from the beginning. I told them about getting a word to step out of the "Worship Pastor" position; about the need that I had to cover those five bills; about the prayer time I had where God assured me that He would meet my need; and about on that same day God mustered up a $891.00 offering for the bills that had not even arrived yet. When I got to the window, I turned my left palm toward Mr. Burrell and told him the whole story too. I asked him, "Is God at work?" Mr. Burrell said, "There's something going on!"

I paid for the money orders. I held on to the money orders rather than doing what was necessary to mail the bills because I wanted to go tell people about the miracle. I drove straight to church. I found Pastor David and Ann in the office. Pastor David could see the excitement in my eyes. I asked him, "Do you remember I told you I needed money to pay those five bills?" He said, "Yeah." "Do you remember how much the offering was?" He said, "Yeah." "Look!" I turned my left palm up so he could see it. Pastor David said, "To the dollar." There were no words that could be said without me bursting out into tears and Pastor David intuitively knew it. He shot me with a finger pistol, with a "there you go!" kind of look on his face. I shot him back with tears welling up in my eyes and rushed out the door.

I went home and found Leslie working in the kitchen. I walked up behind her and said, "Les. Remember the offering was $891.00?" She said, "Yes." "Look!" I turned my left palm to her face. Her jaw dropped and she said very soberly, "Well! Shut my mouth.

Literally." Leslie mourned over the things she said when she doubted God on Saturday night. The good thing was, she had come to her senses that same night and had resolved that the Lord would meet our need. Leslie went through her reverent "I am a man of unclean lips" reaction that I had already gone through at the post office. We were both able to relish the goodness of God. We were both very excited about our prospects for the future. Our "financial" state certainly had not changed, but it <u>was</u> certain that God was at work.

This is one of many stories of how God has confirmed that He is working in and through us by meeting our needs in very obvious miracles. It happens so many times that everybody around us recognizes that they are not coincidences. Many people asked me during the previous year-and-a-half if I had rightly considered my advanced resignation. They knew our financial needs were being met because of that significant part-time salary. I explained to them that it was not a financial decision, it was obedience to God's mandate. After my answer, they realize that you ought not to try to hang on to a ministry position because of pay. It is not too Biblical. Nevertheless, there was a significant shortfall looming up ahead. I knew for certain that God had spoken to me and He told me to step out of that part-time position. I sensed during the time leading up to my final day that

God was pleased with our obedience. He was going to bless not only my family, but Restoration Church as well. I sensed the Lord's pleasure over the whole situation. Deep down, I looked forward to June 1st as a day that God would demonstrate His power. And so again, the Lord glorified Himself for the purpose of broadening His kingdom.

God did not speak to me and tell me that we would get a big financial boon to send us on our way for a Sabbatical. He only assured me that He would meet our financial need. From my lesson where I presumed upon God with the van, I know that I should only rely upon what God has told us. I should only do His bidding. He said, "Stop! Rest! Seek My face!" When I obeyed and sought the Lord's face On June 1st, He showed me that He would take care of my need. He inspired me to document my walk of faith in this book. As I conclude this Episode, I have fulfilled the Lord's post May-2003 tasking. It inspires me with anticipation to ask this question:

"What's next?"

Episode Eighteen

But Wait! There's More!

Stay tuned for the next exciting episode of...

Faith – The Final Frontier

Dedication

This book is dedicated firstly to the Living God who's mercy and grace is boundless. Secondly, to my wife Leslie who has been the model of faith as she submits to the Lordship of Jesus Christ despite her challenging circumstances. Thirdly, to my mother who's effective and fervent prayers have availed much. Fourthly, Brother Leonard Riley, who shepherds the Lord's flock with the love of God the Father. Fifthly, to our more than faithful encouragers and supporters who have partnered with us in our adventures. Some say it was my faith that has brought us so far. I say it is the faithfulness of others that has truly been the means by which God has shown His promises to be true. Lastly, to my humble advocate who, at great personal sacrifice, has wielded the sling while David stands before giants.

About the Author

David Alan Carmichael lives in Hampton, Virginia, with his wife Leslie, and his four children Bethany, Jesse, Isaac, and Abigail (Abby). He has been active in teaching and service ministries since 1985. He served as Worship Pastor at Restoration Church in Hampton, Virginia from May 1, 2000 to May 31, 2003.

In 1997, David started an urban evangelism ministry, Educational Christian Ministries. He provides a free computer course, Introduction to Computers and Word Processing, as a means to meet physical needs and gain opportunities to convey the gospel. He is an effective and dynamic teacher. David also ministers through speaking engagements where he gives motivational messages on the subject of "Faith". His other teaching topics are "Your God, Your Self, Your Government - The Biblical Principles" and "From The Beginning - Genesis:".

(757) 850-2672
1748 Old Buckroe Road
David Hampton Va 23664
Leslie & Abby 304
FaithFrontier@verizon.net